Florida Atlantic University Friends of the Libraries

women of the BOOK

jewish artists jewish themes

judith a. hoffberg

ISBN 0-9706189-0-5

Design: Maritta Tapanainen / Production Assistant: Patrick Percy

Cover: Tatana Kellner: *B-11226: 50 Years of Silence (1992)*

Foreword

We are pleased to have been instrumental in helping to publish a catalog to accompany the "Women of the Book" exhibit, which has been organized by Judith Hoffberg, as it travels around the country. I particularly wish to thank Esther Liu, Florence Kaufelt, Frances Edelman, the Nathan and Marion Crosby Fund, and the Helen Matchett DeMario Foundation for the generous contributions which have helped to make the publication of this catalog possible. When the exhibit was shown here at Florida Atlantic University, it was clear to us that a catalog would enhance the event, in addition to providing the visitors with a permanent recollection of their experience. Now, through the publication of this catalog, future viewers of the exhibit will benefit, and all people can experience something of this exhibit even if they have not seen it in person.

This exhibit joins three strains of particular interest to the FAU Libraries: Women's Studies, Judaica, and the book arts. We have long made Women's Studies a special area of acquisition and visiting scholars have complimented us on the strength of our collections. Our Judaica collections are the largest in Florida, and feature one of the strongest collections of Yiddish-language materials in the world. Our Arthur and Mata Jaffe Collection of Books as Aesthetic Objects is one of the most important collections of artists' books in the country, and its holdings include works by some of the same artists displayed here. It was natural, then, that we would take a special interest in the "Women of the Book" exhibit, and seek to enhance it.

Self-expression through the creation of books as objects of art seems to us, prejudiced as we admittedly are because of our profession of librarianship, to be among the highest forms of human creativity. The skill and inventiveness of the works displayed in this exhibit continue to stretch artistic boundaries and expand the notion of what a "book" might be. Whether the medium be paper, fabric, photo, glass, plastic, or sculpture of various kinds, these books show that there are really no limits for the truly creative mind.

We congratulate the women whose works are highlighted here, and encourage everyone to consider the implications that their books have for the human condition. One need not be a woman, Jewish, or an artist to find these works aesthetically pleasing, challenging, and suggestive. We are proud to be associated with such an enterprise.

William Miller
Director of Libraries
Florida Atlantic University
February 1, 2001

Women of the Book:
Spiritual Journeys, Universal Themes

by Judith A, Hoffberg

Judth A. Hoffberg

For more than thirty years, I have been involved in the field of artist books. Although marginalized in the art world, artist books have found a following and an ever-growing group of artists dedicated to the production of these works of art. Likewise, we have witnessed an important body of critical literature published in the past 10 years, especially in the past five years. I will preface my remarks by explaining that I am not speaking about *livres d'artiste* or about books about art. These are works of art in book form created, for the most part, by visual artists. Since the 1960s, artists have found the new technologies of offset and Xerox, of laser printing and now computer graphics, methods to produce one-of-a-kind and editioned bookworks which are truly attracting collectors, both institutional and private.

The How and the Why

A friend in Philadelphia, noted curator and critic Judith Stein, told me that her sister had been making bookworks for quite a while and asked if I would be interested in contacting her. I agreed and over a period of weeks, we e-mailed each other; finally I convinced her to send me her bookworks for examination. The package arrived, and I spent several hours moved deeply by the subjects covered, among which were: the loss of a child and the book as a healing instrument, the relationship with a family (especially her sister), and the arrival of a chronological landmark and her reaction to it via the book. Her story was unique, but her aesthetics and visual approach rang a bell for me: a clarion call that there was something in the air among Jewish women artists, that although closeted or segregated as "the other," they had much to say via their bookworks, so much in fact that perhaps I would find enough Jewish artists throughout the world who would be willing to participate in an exhibition.

I returned the books to Linda Rubinstein but did not forget her. In July 1996, I put out a call on the Internet, asking any Jewish women visual book artists to respond via e-mail. Then I went to New York for a week. Upon my return, there were forty-two answers, the first coming from Belfast, Ireland! As the weeks progressed, the answers increased from New Zealand, Canada, England, Israel, South Africa, Italy and of course around the United States. Women told other women, husbands told their wives, teachers told their artist friends, and by the end of 1996, I started accumulating resumes and slides; I communicated with each and every one of the artists who had responded. I was deeply moved and touched by the response, and as a result, I wanted the artists to know that I was working to find venues for the exhibition, even though all the artists had not yet been selected. Ultimately, there were 90 women from Australia, New Zealand, Canada, England, Italy, Israel, and South Africa, besides the United States.

As an independent curator of artist bookshows, I have found that it has become increasingly difficult to find venues without institutional support. With the narrow focus of Jewish women artists, I went to Jewish institutions, but found that the secular institutions responded much more readily. We finally had an opening venue after eighteen months, and I could call in the bookworks. They kept flowing in and the books revealed much about their ninety creators.

From personal narrative (including family relationships), ritual and liturgy, the Holocaust and history, literature and myth, the books in the exhibition demonstrate how Jewish women artists use the book form to establish their position within Judaism; they also explore the intimacy as well as the universality of the book within the Jewish tradition. With zest and exquisite skill, the books ran the gamut from finely executed artist books by those who have been doing it for many decades (the oldest artist in the show, Miriam Beerman, is eighty years young) to the humorous treatments of liturgy or Jewish daily life. What really moved me most is that all the bookworks had content, something which had not necessarily been the case in the more than a dozen exhibitions I have curated during the past fifteen years. The books had something to say, not simply for themselves but to educate by elucidating issues that are best expressed visually.

In the course of giving orientation tours of the exhibition at least six times a week, I found how I, as curator, became bound with the books and in turn with the Jewish women who created the works of art. I, a Jew, also re-lived my life through these bookworks and questioned cultural identity in art that dealt with the difficulties of Jewish life in America, the haunting pain of the Holocaust, and the cherished aspects of Jewish tradition. My new Jewish "sisters" never hesitated to wrench emotion out of the pages of these books, making each reader/viewer an active participant in every aspect of Jewish life portrayed in these memories.

The Bible

Many of the women commented about the treatment of women in the Bible, sometimes with humor. For instance, Miriam Schaer of Brooklyn in her *Eve's Meditation* ponders the snake and the apple by creating a very flexible snake book in deep purple, which extends and stretches like a "slinky" toy to create a long structure that twists into a snakelike book, with the front and the back adorned with a head of a snake at one end, with glittery jewels and beads, and the tail, jeweled and beaded, on the other as menacing as any snake could be. Each page in this purple snake is in the shape of an apple, die-cut through the pages.

While the above takes a humorous path, Gloria Helfgott takes the Torah form and creates a modern scroll form called *Origins*, which simulates a beautifully boxed Torah with scroll-like pages emanating from the circular form. Stephanie Later illuminates her own manuscript, *Solomon's Song of Songs*, which, laden with jewels and a gold cord, becomes a treasure with sexual demonstrations taken from the original text. Jenni Lukac uses the prophetic *Book of Isaiah* to embed found objects she discovered in Portugal while researching the Jewish colonies there which had escaped Spain

6

during the Diaspora. The book is treated as a container of objects with layers of memories almost as thin as the Bible paper which is used for printing it.

This exhibition expands the notion of Jews as being the "People of the Book," to embrace the Jewish woman as a creative being who is also part of that People. George Steiner, the British critical theorist, notes that following the destruction of the Temple, the reading of Torah became the instrument of exilic survival for the Jews—the literal, spiritual locus of identification. He maintains that the text became the "homeland, rooted in wanderers and nomads, that cannot be destroyed." So it is not unusual to find a seminal piece in the exhibition by one of the youngest artists in the show, Robyn Sassen of South Africa, whose *Identity Text*, an altered South African identification document, is coated in beeswax, including the phrase, "*I am going home*" rubber-stamped in English and in Hebrew across the center spread, in a passport to nowhere (the subjugation of the "others" in South Africa with identification but not identity); the bearer of this particular "passport" has never forgotten her identity. She calls herself in this "passport to nowhere" a "diasporist," which perhaps is the theme of the exhibition. Possibly the smallest piece in the exhibition, but one of the most powerful, the document screams out for freedom so that the artist can assume her true cultural identity.

So too Barbara Magnus has taken her grandfather's German-English dictionary used as a key by these immigrants to open the door to a new society in the United States. She has folded the individual pages of that dictionary to the inside center of each page to create what she describes as "the ultimate dog-eared book." Her *Bible for a New World* honors the book, much used by her grandparents who left their language behind in order to assimilate in a new land.

Additionally, the exhibition itself allowed several of the women to do research, to find their "cultural identity" which had been lost in the shuffle of generations of assimilation. Take, for instance, Elena Siff whose idea for *Rootless: On the Road with my Jewish Half* was a catalyst for a personal journey to trace her father's lineage. She took a toy truck and embellished it with Jewish stars, stamps, and letterheads from the many hotels her traveling grandfather stayed in when he was on the road. Described as a man who "ignored his Jewish identity for all of my life with him," her father sent glowing letters back from his many trips to China and to Europe. The flatbed of the truck holds the story of the family (which has 306 known descendants) from the arrival of the family in 1820 to the United States. Thanks to an uncle, Siff could flesh out the history of her family, half of which is Jewish (her father) and the other half Italian (her mother). Since her father was so nomadic, she really never knew

him well; with this exhibition, she has traced her family history, learned of the many anecdotes and stories, and found the photos and the artifacts that have created a document of a family's life. Her Jewish identity on wheels is the symbol of hope that allows her and her children to know their roots, metaphorically carrying the family into the future.

The Holocaust

In discussing Jewish identity, there are few of these artists who have not been affected by the Holocaust, most personally and others through empathy. One of the most powerful of these in the exhibition is by Tatana Kellner, who was born in Prague in 1950. It is hard to believe that anyone Jewish was born in Prague in 1950, but her parents, who had been sent to the camps, were released and their joy in surviving culminated in the birth of a daughter, Tatana, who later became a bookmaker and a catalyst for women to make artist books, co-founding the Women's Studio Workshop in Rosendale, New York. Kellner has created two stunning book-works, titled *B-11226: Fifty Years of Silence* and *71125: Fifty Years of Silence*. Growing up, Kellner always saw the arms of her father

and her mother, with numbers burned into their skin. She always asked, but they remained silent. Close to the 50th anniversary of the Holocaust, she finally convinced her parents to tell her the story of their internment, but her father insisted that he would do so on his terms, in Czech. Tatana Kellner is bilingual; using her father's handwritten text, as well as her mother's, she created these most profound works of art, with one parent's arms as the focal point of each of the books, molded in paper with the number incised in the skin of the paper. Around those arms, the pages unfold, so that the reader can never avoid the presence of the tattooed arms. Each book is housed in a wooden box with the number burned into the cover of the box. Printed in English and in Czech, these monumental bookworks certainly stand as symbols of the phrase "lest we forget."

Deborah Davidson's family harks back to the 14th century, forced out of Spain in 1492, and settling in Italy. The artist remembers and discourses on the history of her immediate ancestors. Her great-grandmother living in Italy was sent to a camp in that country and wrote letters to the family. Eight letters are extant. Deborah, haunted by those words, dialogues with her ancestor by taking fragments from the letters her great-grandmother wrote in the internment camp and responds in her own voice in a beautifully printed volume called *Voce*. It is a tortured and haunting volume.

Beth Bachenheimer, whose members of her family were decimated in the ovens of the Holocaust, is fortunate to have been the offspring of the only member of the family to be saved. Being a maskmaker as well as a bookmaker, she has accumulated the records of her family for a devastating family history. Using screening and black paint, the experience of turning these loose pages in a black box lets you know about a family that designated Beth's father to be saved via a passport; via Barcelona, he arrived in New York to meet the one other member of the family waiting for him. Thirty-two members of her family were victims of the Holocaust including her grandmother and grandfather. The exhibition gave Bachenheimer permission to re-do a book of her family which she had done a few years ago on the death of her father; this time the book had a different audience and needed to be strengthened and made user-friendly, strong enough to withstand the perusal of hundreds of people. She not only succeeded, she has also moved viewers to tears. Yet there is hope expressed by many artists.

Witness Miriam Beerman, the oldest artist in the exhibition, who was brought up largely with no religion, except the knowledge that she was Jewish. Only with the birth of her sons and their movement toward religious affiliation did she start questioning the reasons for the Holocaust and doing research. The book she submitted to the exhibit, *Survival*, is energetic and vivid, blending the testimonies of such writers as Celan, Primo Levi, and Akhmatova with drawings that have a flamboyant graffiti-like expressionism. Beerman has found some answers to her questions about the Holocaust and her expressionistic, automatic drawing and collage have been guided by those artists and writers who served as witnesses and scribes.

c.j. grossman explores the life of *Frieda Dicker-Brandeis*, who had studied at the Bauhaus, launched an exciting career as an artist, married Paul Brandeis and began an activist life as Hitler rose to power. She and her husband were sent to Terezin, a camp which became the showplace for the Nazi regime, a camp of musicians and artists where concerts were held, art was taught, in a village atmosphere designed to hide the imprisonment of thousands. (The only difference was the stage sets used to impress the officials of the International Red Cross who used to make periodic visits to the camp.) Frieda Dicker-Brandeis, when captured by the Nazis, grabbed her art supplies and used them and countless inventive other supplies to teach the children of Terezin how to draw and paint, how to document their everyday life in the camps. Hiding the drawings and paintings from the officers at hand, those four thousand drawings and paintings became the nucleus of a collection found after the liberation; these works of art, now housed in a museum in Prague and elsewhere, stand witness to the Holocaust. She has been revered by the artist in a book which has been created for the children who come to the exhibition placed on a pedestal-altar, hanging above which is the teacher's "uniform" consisting of a striped dress with a yellow star on the heart side of the bodice, a yellow star on the back. The dress has a dirty

handkerchief on the sleeve, a pair of scissors in its hem, a picture of her husband sewn on the inside hem, some thread, and needles too. This book installation is a tribute to a woman who never forgot that art can be communicated to young people and have lasting value, even under dire circumstances.

Throughout the exhibit are examples of the striped uniforms of those held in concentration camps during World War II. Bachenheimer uses striped material as a backing for some of the documents and photographs in her history of her family's demise; Rochelle Rubinstein, a calligrapher from Canada, created a handwritten Hebrew and English version of the *Book of Lamentations*, which begins with the striped dress of an inmate in the concentration camps and reverts to the clothes as icons, without any reference to the human body, or rather that the bodies have been eliminated; the haunting costumes are still there on exhibit. Read right to left (in Hebrew calligraphy) or left to right (in English), the book is made of felt cover and has a texture and a feeling of skin. The pages that divide the prints pick up the light as if they were bathed with salty tears. The power of the elements of this book is great.

The yellow star, worn by Jews and enforced by the Nazi regime as cultural/religious identification, is a theme and variation throughout the exhibition. Its power becomes more manifest with each contribution. Channa Horwitz has created a Subliminal Star of David in glass. Each of the six panels of glass is drawn with lines which create a pattern of the Jewish Star when put together. On one side, one sees the yellow star embedded in the glass, on the other is a blue Jewish star. Marilyn Rosenberg's *Remember Babi Yar* is an evocation of the thousands of Jews and Russians annihilated at Babi Yar, with the stack of bones and yellow stars emanating from the pages as separate entities and the headlines of newspapers and archives documenting the devastating tragedy. Yellow stars everywhere; these are repeated in Beth Grossman's *Mary of Abraham, Isaac and Jacob*, which is housed in a suitcase turned book in which Grossman has painted a very Jewish-looking Madonna and baby Jesus on the suitcase divider. Inside, on the left, are yellow cloth stars with all the derogatory words one can imagine that Jews have been called, while the stars on the right side of the suitcase book express reverence and praise to the Jewish Mary. The division between Christianity and Judaism is eloquently portrayed by Grossman in referring to the difficult history between Christians and Jews. The suitcase as well reflects the nomadic fate of the Jews, as well as Christians, until they have found a home.

Barbara Milman, a lawyer for twenty-five years, has been pursued by the memory of survival. This history and memorial of survivors whom she has interviewed is now a public demonstration of a group of experiences of survival in Warsaw: an accordion book consisting of linocuts in stark black and white with different texts on each page depicting life as a child in the Warsaw ghetto, then being hidden in the home of Polish friends and finally miraculous escaping from a cattle car one stop before Auschwitz. Milman has become a bookmaker, no longer a working lawyer, and has done a series of accordion books on Prague and Berlin and other cities, with stories about survival.

Gaza Bowen presents a different perspective of the Holocaust. Born in the South, she and her sister grew up with a Catholic neighbor, Kitty Lewis, who lived in the largest house on the block. Kitty and Gaza became fast friends, playing as well as going to school. Kitty had a large bedroom at the top of the house. With access to the attic through Kitty's bedroom closet, the girls used to play out Anne Frank's story. The fantasy was broken only by Kitty's father calling them down to supper. The bookwork, housed in old worn velvet diary covers, is an accordion-fold structure with a die-cut opening in the page depicting the closet with access to the attic, which instead of depicting Kitty's home, now depicts Anne Frank's room in Amsterdam where her whole family was hidden for several years. It is memory that, in the face of the horror of the Holocaust, creates real and present experience, even to children who have only read about it but not suffered it.

Family Relations

Gayle Wimmer, whose father was a "benign tyrant," disappointed her father, for she became an artist. Now a professor at the University of Arizona in Tucson, she documented her father's demise as she watched him die over two years. This "diary" was created after his death on her father's handkerchiefs, on which she screened her own MRI on each handkerchief and then included comments by her father upon her visits with appropriate dates. One can see the slow diminution of her father's anger and his acceptance of his daughter as an artist and a creative human being. The "pages" of this bookwork are the handkerchiefs, heavily starched. It is a moving document, an evocative work of art.

Liliane Lijn's evocation of her mother, in *Her Mother's Voice,* is a combination of feelings, facts, and impressions including documentation of a mother whose strength and exceptional personality have been explored by her artist daughter in a distinctive manner. This is another examination of the artist and her origins. From her parents' fleeing their beloved Europe and arriving in New York, she has gleaned emotional richness, complexity of thought, and intense sense of loss. The book is a combination of high and low technology (using a computer yet printing with a low-end printer on handmade Japanese paper), an oral history presented on the fragile and tactile medium of rice paper mirroring the fragility of human life in general and in particular the fragility of a Jewish woman who lived through the panic years preceding World War II.

Liturgy

With regard to the liturgy, calligraphers have a joyful way of using paper structures to create glorious interpretations of prayers, as in the *Sh'ma* (Hear O Israel, the Lord our G-d, the Lord is One) by Eva-Lynn Ratoff, in a star form, or a miniature book by Roseann Chasman in illuminated calligraphy and papercuts, of the song

Chad Gadya (One Only Kid) sung at the end of the Passover Seder.

Visual artists who know their prayers have also reacted to the one prayer orthodox men say each morning: "Blessed art thou, O Lord our G-d, King of the Universe, who has not made me a woman." In response to that statement, both Carol Hamoy and Robbin Ami Silverberg have developed feminist approaches. Hamoy's family comes from the garment district of New York, so she has created a bejeweled volume (done with decorations found in the garment district in gilt) with the double spread subverted statement: "Thank you Lord for making me a woman who is an artist!"

Alisa Golden, known for her Never the Mind Press, has created *Gateway,* which is a reaction to the Sabbath candlesticks which to the artist appear to be pillars, marking the entrance to a world separate from the work-week. The poem, which is printed on this tunnel book, is about lighting the candles, celebrating the connection with her ancestors and Jews around the world. The print is a shaped text, simulating the candlesticks themselves.

Alyssa Salomon in her *Diaspora Menorah* develops the theme for Chanukah, the Feast of Lights, by creating a bookwork that is copper-coated, folds up like a book, and is incised with the prayer for lighting the candles during the eight days of Chanukah. When you open the book, there are holders for the eight candles and the Shamus, or the candle with which you light the others night after night. It is a book that is functional and provides a memory of a hasty escape during the Diaspora, when performing the ritual was even more meaningful but clandestine.

Myth and Reality

Sophia Rosenberg's *Lilith Scroll* brings us full circle to the investigation of the Biblical first woman Lilith, who seems to the artist to embody all the things that have been exiled or edited out of religious Judaism: the feminine, the sexual, the psychic, the mystical, the dark. An aura of fear surrounded her and a wealth of amulets was designed to keep her away. But who was she? Biblically, she was the first wife of Adam, the two together being made in the image of G-d. She refused to lie beneath him and fled the garden to take residence beside the Red Sea where she is said to have given birth to demons.

As a performance artist, Rosenberg began to explore Lilith in herself, costuming herself and dancing. On one of these occasions, a photographer friend took the photographs for the scroll. The artist wrote poems as well, which are the written remnants of the exploration. Incorporating the photographs, poems, and handmade papers, Rosenberg discovered that the form of the scroll, sacred to the Jews and alluding to the Torah, was a perfect situation to create a space for Lilith and in turn for the dark, female, sexual, mystical part of herself. Reclaiming some of the power behind the taboos regarding women, blood, sexuality, and death, the *Lilith Scroll* is a dramatic exploration and collaboration of the feminist approach to an interpretation of a Biblical tract. It allows the reader/viewer to lift the veils over each of the poems and discover who Lilith really is to the artist.

It has been a remarkable journey for this exhibit and for me. The women I have learned to know through the electronic and postal media have been "the other" for so long. They first of all are women, secondly they are Jewish, and thirdly they are artists. That would be a triple negative in this culture. But, their art has sustained them and allowed them to express themselves in many ways. Always creative, always breaking the mold, these women have found a way to tell about themselves and their ethnic and spiritual culture in very specific ways. Taunted by prejudice and separateness, these women have courageously surpassed hurdles and have created remarkable works of art in a medium known so well to their "people": the book. That familiar form of book has been expanded to incorporate not only new technology but also the old structures. As a result, these women have created their own bridge, their own windows to their souls and to their spirits. I salute them as catalysts for allowing a much larger audience to know and participate in their creativity and their culture.

Judith A. Hoffberg
Curator

Prayers Made Silent

Dear Judith:

Imade it my business yesterday to drive to Kutztown University to see for myself your extraordinary exhibition *Women of the Book*! Ah, the range; Ah, the insight!

You have gathered together a wonderfully rich variety of bookforms which open upon the historical pain and wisdom of both post-Holocaust Judaism and of women as daughters and mothers…it is a memorial encased, locking thoughts and feelings in, and drawing us as audience through the leaves of prayer and memory and contact of hair and stone, through astonishing tearing apart of bibles, reminscences of Torah scrolls and katubahs, confrontations with prayers denying the rights, even existence, of women, remnants of clothing and yellow(ed) stars of fear and hatred as identity, and bodies turned to piles of bones and bones and bones! The books become a burial monument, and in my mind they become a pyre, a connection with the Bible in which each word is a source of flamed inspiration, a holy point where the spirit does reside.

In many ways, this exhibit extends the role of women artists' bookmaking in the autobiographical direction in which it always seems to go…art as a search for and acknowledgment of identity, encased, with skill and signs [the symbols, the threads, the founds, both historical and redolently around], stitched with both consciousness and care(fully), most often very tactile, cautious, valuable, present (by weight and shape and aesthetic force), and, of course, extraordinarily inventive in technique; they are a turning inward, an in-closing, a holding with-in, a privacy, a private place/space, and thus a sadness and a closure, a not being seen, an historical documentation of documents, a re-searing of a wound after first re-opening it. These are acts held. Prayers made silent. Because of the subject, however, it is as if the viewer/reader were standing in history at a huge gravesite davenning [because that is all history allows us to do]. I am re-awared of the marginality of artmaking in this moment of culture…these books also fall somehow into a Borgesian mirror whirled…they are a piece of a large circle which includes men of the book, both horrified artists and orthodoxed world-enclosers, and fascists and commodifiers…

Your extraordinary articulation of a portion of that whole humanity is a great contribution…brava brava. I am reduced, finally, to silent prayer only.

David Cole
(1939-2000)

Editor's Note: David Cole was an extraordinary visual poet and painter, one whose energy gave energy to all around him. He made a very great effort to see the exhibition before he became gravely ill with respiratory disease, which finally took him from us this year. We mourn his passing each day.

Itinerary

Finegood Art Gallery, Bernard Milken Jewish Community Center
West Hills, CA
23 November 1997 - 11 January 1998

Sharadin Art Gallery,
Kutztown University
Kutztown, PA
4 February 1999 - 7 March 1999

University of Pennsylvania Special Collections Library
Kamin Gallery, Van Pelt-Dietrich Library
Philadelphia, PA
A selection of 48 pieces from the show
6 June 1999 - 6 August 1999

Janice Charach Epstein Museum/Gallery
West Bloomfield, MI
14 October - 21 November 1999

University of Arizona Museum of Art
Tucson, Arizona
12 December 1999 - 27 January 2000

Florida Atlantic University
Boca Raton, FL
13 February - 26 March 2000

Brattleboro Museum of Art
Brattleboro, VT
19 May - 30 July 2000

Southwest Missouri State University
Springfield, MO
25 October - 1 December 2000

Jewish Community Center of Greater Minneapolis
and Minnesota Center for Book Arts
Minneapolis, MN
25 March - 19 May 2001

Ita Aber

The Greek letter Gamma design is known to have been used on Jewish women's clothing as a way of distinguishing women's clothing from men's in the Pre-Christian period. The men's symbol was a Greek letter Eta. Evidence of this is found in the murals of the Dura Europus frescoes that were excavated by Yale University as well as in the archeological evidence found at Masada and at Bar Kokhba's cave of the year 132 C.E. There are mosaics in Italy and the same symbols are used on women's and men's sarcophagi.

Gamma Book · mixed media · 1997

Joyce Abrams

Born in a Fire · laser printed · 1994

When I was in elementary school, my friend Mark asked me to marry him. I said that I couldn't because we were not the same religion. I was Jewish; he was Kosher.

Although raised without Jewish traditions, such as religious observances or knowledge of Yiddish or Hebrew, I am plainly and essentially a Jew. This identity sadly has been sharpened by an awareness of the Diaspora, the Holocaust and ever-present anti-Semitism. It is my belief in One, as well as in the ethical, intellectual, questioning, and creative aspects of Judaism, that affect me and my work.

For me the artist's book is the perfect medium to disclose ideas within an intimate format. This process of assembling visual material with words draws on my experience as a painter, sculptor, and filmmaker. The sequence of pages is like the scenes of a film. The pace, which is influenced by the amount of information on each page, supports the narrative. At the same time, the design and scale emphasize the overall theme and enhance the personal nature of the book.

Not shown: *The Legacy* · 1994.

Melinda Smith Altshuler

As a granddaughter of Jewish immigrants, I have never really known what objects were brought from Europe by my family or what was acquired as an inexpensive used item to recreate a home, or history. All objects were treated with respect and as precious.

I like to draw on these lessons of object loss and found, as a memorial for family member loss and rebirth in regards to the stamina of my people and our heritage. The use of found books and objects in my work does not fulfill a need to create a history at this point but there is that magical moment of unveiling odd treasures that I still thrive on.

The White Album · Victorian photo album, found objects, acrylic · 1997

Our Friends · Victorian photo album, found objects, acrylic · 1997

Lynne Avadenka

I combine words and images to create a single visual statement. The ongoing theme of my work is communication, both visual and through text. Much of my subject matter is inspired by Judaic themes and my goal is a synthesis presenting traditional subjects in a contemporary context. The challenge is to preserve the spirituality of the material while connecting it to the present.

Not shown: *Compassion* · 1991.

An Only Kid · letterpress · 1990

Living with Memory · plastic, acrylic, photos · 1997

Beth Bachenheimer

My father died in January 1997 from heart failure. During the grieving process, I created this artwork. Growing up with family memories and feelings surrounding the Holocaust, this art book relieved the burden, which I carried on my shoulders for many years of my life. I am the last of my immediate family. I am the sole survivor. As an artist this is my way of expressing so many unsaid feelings and honoring the family I have never met.

Marion A. Baker

In 1978 at the Women's Building I learned letterpress printing. From that time I have been obsessed with learning about and making artist books. *Women of Genesis* (now out of print) was my first publication. I like the human quality of these early women. Not saints, they were curious, proud, jealous, scheming, and helpful.

Women of Genesis · letterpress, photo engravings · 1980

Little Orphan Anagram · Granary Books · letterpress, watercolor, gouache · 1997

Susan Bee / Charles Bernstein

I have rarely dealt directly with Jewish themes. My work has instead been a personal exploration of my encounter with American culture, as well as with abstraction, gender, and aesthetic issues. But because of my background I have always come at American culture at an oblique angle. I have always felt somewhat outside of the mainstream as a Jewish woman and as the daughter of artists. My mother was brought up in a Jewish orphanage in Berlin. The whole orphanage was moved to Jerusalem when she was a teenager. This lucky stroke of fate saved her from extermination. So in a sense, the title of *Little Orphan Anagram* refers to her.

Miriam Beerman

I was born into an assimilated Jewish family in New England. My religious leanings were vague and spread out in all directions from Quaker to Catholic. It was not until I met my husband Julian Jaffe (and his family, devoted to scholarly conservative Judaism) that I learned what it meant to be a Jew. My son Bill is a truly devoted Jew, observing the Sabbath and studying Talmud every week.

The mystical aspects of Judaism interest me. Since the middle forties, when I heard rumors of the Holocaust, I have been haunted by history. A great portion of my life work as a painter has borne the weight of this tragedy.

Survival · drawing, collage on paper · 1997

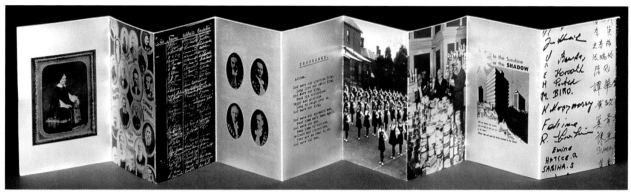

Collected Histories · card paper · 1995   Courtesy: Karyn Lovegrove Gallery, Los Angeles

Lauren Berkowitz

(Australia)

My work deals directly and indirectly with my Jewishness. There is a particular relation to the Holocaust, an obsessiveness and fascination with archives, lists of names, monuments of celebration and commemoration.

In 1993 I was living and working in New York City. While I was preparing my master's thesis in the form of an artist's book, I showed a professor my work for his opinion. He looked carefully through the pages stopping at the place where I had photocopied the listings of all the Berkowitzes in the New York City telephone book. He said in a knowing voice, you must be Jewish, all Jews are obsessed with locating their extended Jewish family and relatives through the telephone book wherever they travel around the world. My professor's comments seemed very perceptive. I did realize my family had a habit of always looking up all the Berkowitz and other family surnames. Knowing that they had almost certainly been forcibly displaced in the past due to persecution, this is particularly true around the events of World War II and the Holocaust.

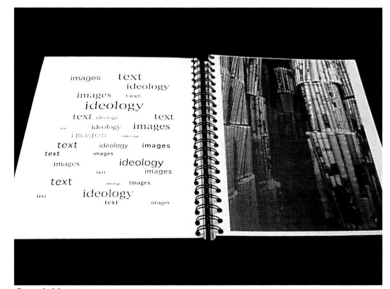

Recyclable · recycled paper · 1995   Courtesy: Karen Lovegrove Gallery, Los Angeles

23

Gaza Bowen

The Secret Game · laser printing, velvet, brass · 1997
Courtesy: Couturier Gallery, Los Angeles

The history of my life cannot be separated from the lives of others. The lives that have touched me have become me. Neither can my story be separated from the culture, environment, or period in which I live. Being born Jewish in the South during World War II presented me with a unique set of experiences. My memories serve as the truth of my experiences.

The Secret Game is one of those memories. It tells the story of two young girls in the early 1950s and their self-invented game of "Anne Frank." The book is illustrated with simple line drawings reminiscent of children's school books from that era. The text similarly evokes a secure, cheery American middle class.

In addition to personal memory, *The Secret Game* speaks of the moment of encounter between two cultures: how a young, naive America experienced the Holocaust during Saturday matinee newsreels and the 1952 publication of *The Diary of Anne Frank*.

Terry Braunstein

My maiden name, Malikin, is not a common one, and it was understood that the customs officials that welcomed grandfather Morris into America had misunderstood the pronunciation of the surname. However, when my niece went on the Internet two years ago to see what she could find under her last name, she got back a response from an organization calling itself "Schtetlinks." Its contents startled the entire family. The document she received listed people from a small town in Russia, who had been rounded up and shot by the Nazis, and there was the name "Malikin" on it, three separate times. The family had always suspected that something horrible had happened to their grandfather's family. He, and three of their other grandparents, had escaped to the United States when programs in Russia were regular occurrences. The Cossacks would ride through the tiny Jewish shtetl, where they had lived, and kill anyone in their way. He had left when drafted into the Russian army, at a time when every young Jewish male that was drafted was sent to the frontline, and often never seen again. And then, there was World War II, and the Nazis, who came through the Russian Pale, killing whatever Jews were left.

Still, they were not prepared for these notes, and this list, and their name, three times. They were not prepared for the numbers in each family and the ages of each person. I suddenly saw my great grandfather and great grandmother, my great aunts and uncles, and all my Malikin cousins. It was two years later, when I visited Ellis Island, and photographed a tailor shop, not that different from my grandfather's in the Bronx, that I saw the book *Shot on the Spot* come together—my grandfather's new start in America, juxtaposed with the horrors he had left behind.

Not shown: *Theater or Life?* • 1983.

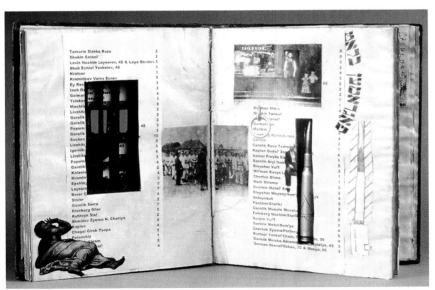

Shot on the Spot • mixed media, unique book • 1999

Jo-Anne Brody

This book is the history of our family and heritage. It contains our names in Hebrew and Yiddish for at least three generations. It is a reminder of our roots. It is a Ketuba in clay for my daughter who was eight when we moved to Israel for three years. She and I learned Hebrew. She, of course, always spoke better than I did; she dreamed in Hebrew. I became *Eema*, her father *Abba*. And now she is married. I wanted to share the stories of our experiences with the next generation. So I talk to my daughter of my grandparents' immigrant stories; of our cousin's experiences in the Holocaust; of my parents' lives, and of my life and hers. I want to remind her of her wisdom and her triumphs. And I want to celebrate our lives and the promise of her child to be. So I speak in our secret language, woman to woman, *ani l'at*. Through this book I entrust my daughter with our family's heritage—past, present and future.

Book of Women · stoneware, oxides, glaze · 1997

Chad Gadya · papercutting, hand-lettering · 1997

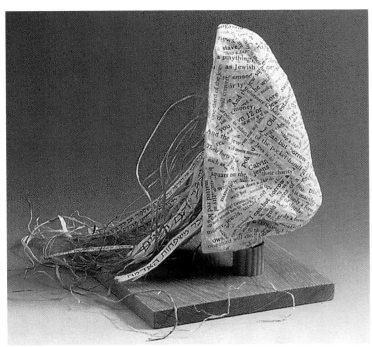

Stuffed Nose · paper maché, raffia · 1998

Rose Ann Chasman

What being Jewish means to me and my work? Everything! Questioners will assume that my Judaism represents constriction—that, as some artists do, I value limits placed on the chaotic forces of my creativity. I must sometimes insist forcibly: Judaism is the *source* of my creativity. It's where the good ideas hang out! Traditional Jewish life patterns and texts are a boundless sea—a dance of meaning.

I work in traditional Jewish book arts—calligraphy, papercutting, and ketuba making, pushing the boundaries with innovative materials and techniques, and subjects drawn from a life-long highly personal dialog with the classic texts. Hebrew letter forms are an important element in my work.

Deborah Davidson

*V*oce is a book that is part of a large body of work that is concerned with my family history. The books are the most formal of my work, but also the most personal. They lead me not only to exploring my family's history for its own richness, but also to dealing with larger historical and cultural issues. The poems are inspired by eight letters written by my great-grandmother, Gemma Servadio, from an internment camp in Italy in 1944. She was killed at Auschwitz two months later. Excerpts from the letters also appear in the book, so there is a mingling of the two voices. What began as a way of coming to terms with a specific and small story evolved to encompass issues not only of the Holocaust, but also of being Jewish, of memory, both personal and collective.

My response to the political is the personal. My deepest wish is that somehow my work could save Gemma, and more modestly, that I could bury her properly. I am trying to find her, to listen to her, and to honor her. The book aims to be a leap of faith, a way of tracing memory, a way of making visceral and visible that which is evanescent.

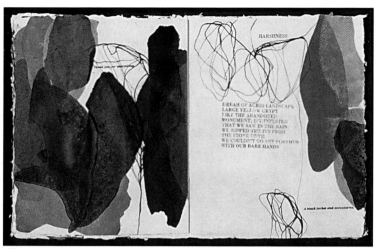

Voce · handmade paper, ink, monotype, Xerox transfer · 1995

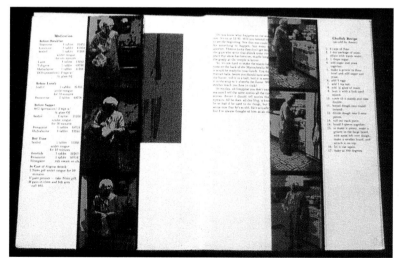

No Soup, Just Matzo Balls · photo silkscreen, offset printing · 1985

Abbe Don

My great-grandmother Annie Shapiro told stories to anyone who would listen as she weaved in and out of the past and present, the old country and America, English and Yiddish. *No Soup, Just Matzo Balls* is an interactive book that tries to capture Annie's storytelling style with pieces of oral history, photographs, and text fragments. The pages of the book are layered with dye cuts and folded pouches so that the act of reading the book both reveals and conceals different stories similar to the experience of looking through Annie's scrapbook. The book is a limited edition of 25, printed in Baskerville type on Starwhite Cover paper with 20 hand silkscreened photographs.

WOMEN of the **BOOK**

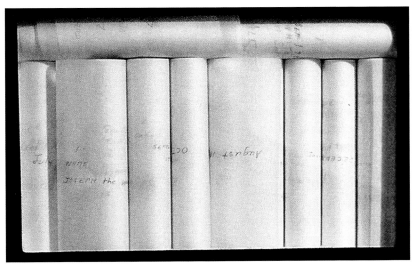

Twelve Months/Sacred Offerings · pencil on 12 vellum scrolls, specimen box · 1997

Evidence of Passover/8 Matzohs · Matzoh, typewriter ribbon, India ink, varnish · 1997

Barbara Drucker

I first went to Greece 12 years ago in order to experience the Greek Easter religious celebrations and rituals firsthand. I am always searching for the connections between psychology, religion and art-making. All deal with soul, feelings and understandings. In my artwork I try to express my feelings and understandings about living and being human. Through my first trips to Greece, I learned more about Christianity, its current practice and the meaning it holds for a whole group of people, and I learned more about its source, Judaism. I continue to explore my relationship to both sets of beliefs, and feel nurtured by and outside of both.

Johanna Drucker

I have a strong sense of identification with my Jewish cultural heritage, rather than a commitment to Jewish religious practice. Even in the Reform tradition in which I was raised, the patriarchal bias of Jewish texts, law, and cultural norms was painfully and overwhelmingly clear to me. The feminist rewriting of the old testament which initiates *The History of the/my Wor(l)d* acknowledges and subverts that patriarchal tradition. The long association of the Word with Truth and the Image with the Flesh, and the negative characterization of the latter within Judeo-Christian and Classical Western culture, persist as fundamental features of contemporary criticism. The interrogation of these basic notions within a feminist perspective has provided a point of departure for a number of my artist's bookworks *Through Light and the Alphabet* and *The Word Made Flesh* as well as the one exhibited here.

The History of the /my World · offset interior, letterpress covers · 1995

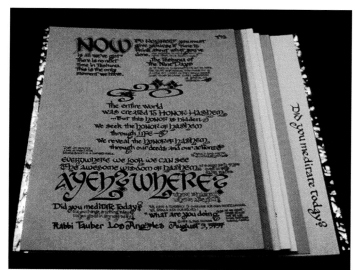

Grab hold of Life and Fill it with Holiness! · Notes on Jewish Meditation from lectures by Rabbi Elchonon Tauber · mixed media · 1997

Rae Ekman

The Power of the Alef Bet:
A Calligrapher's Story

I was part of the wounded generation of Jews after the Holocaust who either had not formal training at all, or were brought up in spiritually empty congregations. Thank G-d, I learned about some of the Jewish holidays and customs, how to lead an ethical life, and how to read the Alef Bet. I was bat mitzvah and "confirmed" and then I had nothing whatever to do with Judaism for 10 years. I searched into all kinds of other spiritual paths but I didn't get trapped into anything.

One Friday night I was "sufi" dancing. This particular group took chants from various religions and combined them with circle dances for world peace. The group began to chant the Shema, which I barely remembered, but I

Evelyn Eller

The book format is a natural form to express my ideas on memory, travel, language and nature. Lately I have been using the book as a sculptural object in which I combine disparate materials. Many of my books incorporate wooden boxes, photographs, reproductions, maps, music, as well as print from newspapers and magazines.

Not shown: *Jerusalem Pilgrim* · 1997.

Recalling Another Era · mixed media collage, Xerox, bookcloth · 1997

realized that they were doing it all wrong. Then I met up in the circle dance with a fellow I knew who was also Jewish, so I said: "Shabbat Shalom." He said, "Oh yeah. Friday is Shabbat, isn't it?" That scared me. I thought, what if I get so far away from Judaism that I don't even remember which day of the week is Shabbat?

Soon after, I saw a flyer on a kiosk at Humboldt State University, where I was studying art. It was written in Hebrew and I stood there a long time with tears spilling over, trying to remember how to decipher the letters. That was my turning point. From that moment on, the Alef Bet led me back in, letter by letter. I was just finishing up my first class in calligraphy and I arranged with my professor, Reese Bullen, to do an independent study in Hebrew calligraphy. I copied prayers out of the Siddur and studied Rabbi Aryeh Kaplan's books and whatever I could find on the mystical Alef Bet.

In 1993, I decided to try keeping Shabbos. I wanted to see if I experienced as much inner conflict by giving up the things I thought were essential, as I experienced by doing things that I knew violated Shabbos. It only took three Shabbats before all of my inner conflict was resolved and I was committed. Naturally, writing was the last and hardest to let go.

In June of 1997, by the grace of G-d, I moved to the wonderful Torah community of Los Angeles. There are many gifted teachers of Torah in Los Angeles, and I go to as many shiurim as I can. These pages, and over 300 others from learning in New York, San Francisco, and Israel are "notes" that I take while sitting in the class. Rabbi Tauber teaches classes on Sunday nights at 9:00 p.m. at Rabbi Citron's Shul, Ahavas Yisroel, 731 No. La Brea Ave. You are invited to come and learn. May we all be inspired to learn and spread the light of Torah, one to another, from this world to the World-to-Come.

Dorothy Field (Canada)

I grew up in an assimilated family in New York in a town were being Jewish seemed totally normal. In that atmosphere, I thought very little about my Jewish identity. When I moved to a farm in rural Canada, I found myself living at the edge of the Diaspora. People said to me, "Oh, there was a Jew here once." I realized that despite my scant Jewish grounding, I felt Jewish and I would have to educate myself to figure out what that meant. For me, the core orientation of my Jewishness grows out of the idea of *tikkun olam*, the repair of the world. In my work, both visual and written, I try to speak out even when it feels risky and to work towards integration of the shadow side, the Other, the Jew, on a personal and political level.

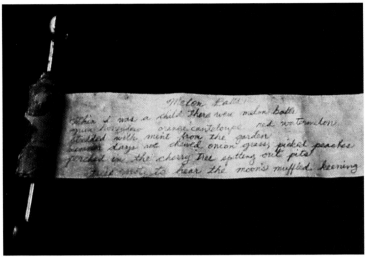

Melon Ball Megillah · mixed media · 1996

Libros de los Desterrados · handmade paper, amate cutouts · 1996

Diane Fine/Beth Fine Kaplan *The Moonkosh Press*

The source of *Forever and Ever* is the desire to understand the role that Judaism plays in coping with breast cancer in our family. Since my sister Beth's diagnosis three and a half years ago, we have often spoken of the unanswered and unanswerable questions we have encountered through this experience. The metaphor of the sealed box as container for the answers we cannot know led us to explore the message, ritual, and history of tefillin. We were unfamiliar with the practice because, as women, we were excluded from that obligation. As we read and talked to our rabbis and to each other, we found wonder, comfort, and a shared challenge in learning to wear tefillin. Our study, and this book, has enlightened us with its message. There is healing in that message.

Forever and Ever · letterpress in a mixed media box · 1997

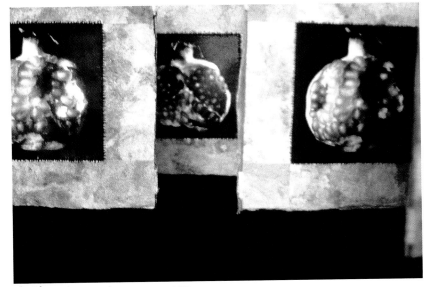

Inside · photography, paper · 1997

Rose-Lynn Fisher

Just when it seems there is nothing more—the end of the road—you peel away this apparent evidence of completion and discover a fresh new field of possibility and beauty, abiding like a buried treasure. For me life is like a pomegranate.

Faiya Fredman

d. & h.r.'s desert · mixed media · 1997

All of the past is part of the present is part of the future. I am a product of history, an accumulation from the beginning of Time, a unique combination for this moment, one that will disintegrate and reform into another in the future carrying the residue of many pasts with it. The sum of the Jewish pasts in me formed a questioning, inquisitive mind that keeps rolling over on itself asking the next question and then the next and the next...I am part of the tradition.

Man at Work · paper, acetate (silkscreened) · 1976-86

Pnina Gagnon (Canada/Israel)

Man at Work is an artist's book written with Hebrew characters, but it contains words in Yiddish, Arabic and Hebrew. It consists of notations taken by the artist in 1974 on a small building site in Haifa, Israel where it is frequent to hear Jewish and Arabic workers communicating in these three languages. In recent years Russian and Rumanian are added to the construction sites as new buildings are erected everywhere and newcomers with foreign workers are added to the regular workforce. This situation in which an Arab worker will use Yiddish words in his workplace is probably unique to Israel.

The 24 images are serigraphs on acetate, separated by four prints on paper, showing the artist's father, Moshe Cohen, who was a pioneer builder, in the process of building a wall. The artist describes in the handwritten scrolled text the different steps it takes to construct: the digging of the foundation; the preparation of the cement and the different materials necessary for the work; the building of the wall with beton blocks; the laying down of the cement and of the finishing layer in stucco; the construction of a roof and of a floor. At the end there is a glossary of the most frequently used terms.

Vered Galor

Days of My Life · offset, ed. 100 · 1980

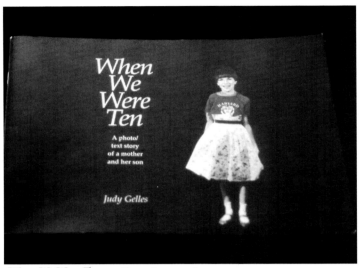

When We Were Ten · offset, photographs, text · 1997

Judy Gelles

Being Jewish has been, and is, an integral part of my persona. Growing up in a French Canadian mill town in New Hampshire during the 1950s was difficult for me. I was afraid to admit to anyone that I was Jewish. It was my secret. Anti-Semitism was hidden, and at the same time it was pervasive. In my book *When We Were Ten*, I decided to put a Jewish label on my sixteen-year-old portrait and finally openly admit to my Jewish heritage. Many readers have expressed to me their discomfort with the label. Yet, for the first time, I am finally at home with myself, and am excited to be in a show with other Jewish artists.

Ruth Ginsberg-Place

Jews have a reputation as urban dwellers. Indeed, this was my history and geography growing up in Brooklyn. As a child my Jewish neighbors talked about "going to the country," a place I could only imagine. I sought out a park nearby, barren and raggedy as it was, to create "the country" for myself within my neighborhood. Later I discovered even more beautiful parks in my city and in the city of Boston where I moved. Wherever I go, I go to parks. My book documents this life-long involvement.

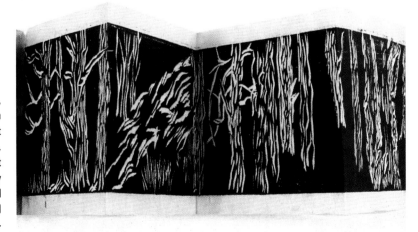

In the Arboretum · woodblock prints, Rives BFK paper · 1996

Sylvia Glass

I use the humblest of materials in my books, including rocks, fossils, twigs, and a myriad of found objects. This process suggests a strong human presence.

Each page is made of 7 layers of muslin. Then four pages are sewn together to create the book. The surface of the cloth is aged, scarred and abraded. Sometimes objects are placed between the layers, sometimes they are partly hidden.

I hope to set up a dialogue and an intimate connection with the viewer. I want my work to appear to be archeological finds from ancient people to suggest their aspirations. In these particular books I hope to suggest the survival and history of Israel.

Matters of the Spirit · mixed media · 1992

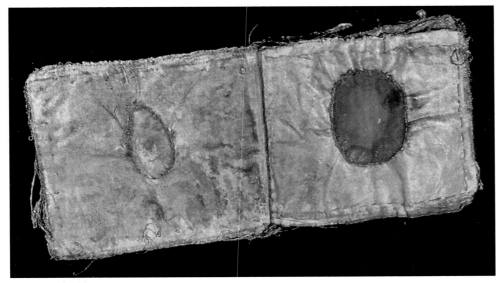

Whisper of a Memory · mixed media · 1993

Alisa Golden

Since 1983, I have written, designed, printed and bound more than fifty editions with approximately ten percent devoted to distinctly Jewish themes. *Gateway* was born when I saw that the Shabbat candlesticks stand as pillars, marking the entrance to a world separate from the work-week: every Friday night after I light the Shabbat candles, I do no business, handle no money, and devote the day to my family. The poem about lighting the candles celebrates the connection with my ancestors and Jews around the world.

Gateway · letterpress, torn paper tunnel book center · 1992

Mary of Abraham, Isaac and Jacob · mixed media · 1996

Passages · mixed media · 1996

c.j. grossman

There was a time when I had read a few books on the Holocaust and thought I had read it all. I was overwhelmed with the depths of the inhumanity with which one human could treat another. Then I began reading about the Holocaust in earnest. I didn't expect to find answers so much as I wanted to know the stories. I wanted to know not only the horrors, but the trials, the tribulations, the sacrifices, the inventiveness, the creativity, and the courage with which people lived their lives in that terrible tragic time.

That is how I came upon the story of Friedl Dicker-Brandeis, a Jewish woman, an artist, a teacher, and very definitely a heroine. I was so moved by her life that it became a story that I wanted to tell, in order to keep her inspiration and memory alive. And, as Elie Wiesel says, even if you were not involved in the Holocaust itself, if you tell the stories and educate people, then you also bear witness. And so I am a witness, and if you repeat the stories, you will be too.

Beth Grossman

My art focuses on the relationship between my heritage, community, and environment. I seek to involve community, draw upon Jewish history, establish a connection to the present, and demonstrate hope to the future. I begin by collecting oral histories and found objects that tell a story about a particular time, place or community. I add my marks, questions and message to the commonplace objects creating new stories which are connected to the cultural symbolism of the objects and to the people who used them before me.

Friedl Dicker-Brandeis, a Flame that will Never be Extinguished
Book: goatskin, paper, brass screws • Dress: cotton dress, paper, yarn, photo, pencil, metal and string • 1995-6

Carol Hamoy

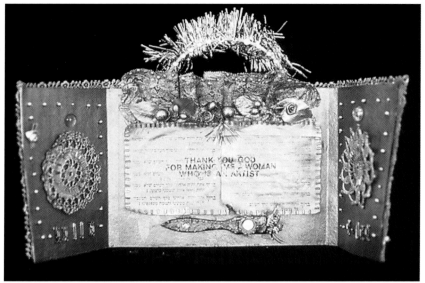

Morning Prayer · handmade paper, beads, lace, tinsel, metal glass, paintbrush, Xerographic image, acrylic · 1995

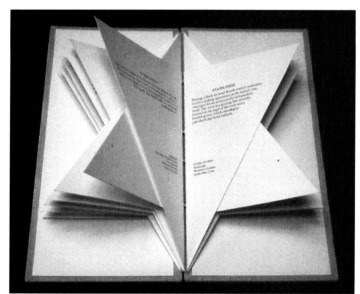

Visions of Golda · letterpress, hand sewn binding, linen thread, silk covered boards · 1999   Purgatory Pie Press · production

Dedication and commitment to developing and making my art has always taken precedence over everything else in my life. My passion for women's history is rooted in my childhood, where, as a first generation girl-child, few expectations (except traditional ones like marriage and family) and opportunities were available. I felt invisible and unimportant. And, perhaps because of those circumstances, I now view life through a feminist lens. My interests lie in issues of central importance to women and my pieces are visual narratives celebrating women from the spiritual and the cultural past. Although the work is often gender-based, I feel ethereal messages and universal truths are expressed going beyond gender. Transferring artifacts from my family's work in the garment industry (fabric, lace, tulle, beads, etc.) into my media, I explore themes of female identity, family values, spirituality, and true friendship. In those of my works with Jewish themes, I strive to make visible the invisible part of the "children of Israel" by telling the stories and legends of these powerful and wonderful women. In doing so, I hope to raise the consciousness of the people who view the works.

Not shown: *God's Books* · 1995.

Gloria Helfgott

In the Beginning · acrylic, acrylic modeling paste, glass beads on Arches cover paper · 1997

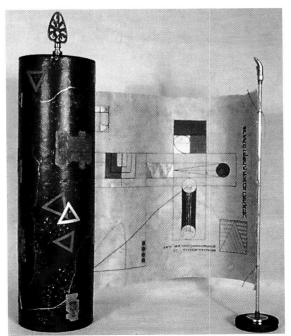

Origins · mixed media (acrylic, brass, rubber) · 1997

In the beginning was "the Word," the theme of the book. Each of the folds has a cutout of the first word of the five books of Moses and the "tablets" represent the texts of the Pentateuch. The embellishment of the page is a metaphor for the reverence of the bible as sacred literature.

Judy Hoffman

I was always making things, as far back as I can remember. Playing with my brother in the woods, I'd construct homes among the trees with string, twigs, bark, anything we could find. There I found the beginnings of my gut impulses, a world of ideas and my wonder of nature.

I still find my spiritual center through my hands. Visual images pop into my head. I translate them and work through the touching. The act of making paper, twisting, gluing, tearing, mixing colors, becomes an active meditation an entrance into a place of mental peace where my visual thinking emerges and often surprises me.

The works I have made directly exploring prayer and Jewish themes (e.g. *Siddur: Blessing on Seeing the Wonders of the Trees, The Whole World is a Narrow Bridge*) are inspired by the Jewish feminist community's movement to reinterpret and invent forms of ritual and expressions of spirituality. They are created to search for and deepen my connections to Jews and Judaism.

I am wild for nature—the changing colors of leaves, flickering sunlight touching tree bark, the lace of worn shells. These are miracles—the webs made by tree branches and vines the deep glowing blue of morning glory petals. I bless them as they bless me.

Siddur: Blessing on Seeing the Wonders of the Trees · artist-made paper · 1997

The Whole World is a Narrow Bridge · monotype, collage, stamping · 1992

Channa Horwitz

I am a spiritual being in search of truth. My place of worship is within and I am one with all.

Subliminal Star of David · glass, metal plaka, gold paint · 1997

Eternal Orb · wood, wire, book, ink · 1993

Sandra Jackman

The book is my subject
 Reading is my inspiration.
 The blank page is my passport—my freedom to journey wherever...
 The blank page need not be made of paper.
 The transfer of information need not be made of words.
 An artist's book need not be a facsimile.
 Often I translate the book into a sculptural construction—a composition that suggests...

Jacqueline Jacobs

I was born in Chile, a second generation Jew. My Jewish education was lacking as my mother wanted to be totally modernized and rejected her Jewish Heritage. Only when I met my husband in the US, also a physician, did I decide to stay. This was a turning point in my Judaism as it was then that my interest in learning was rekindled.

I consider myself fortunate to have a dual career involving the Healing and the Visual Arts. Science and Art are intertwined, they both deal with Life as a creative force justifying our presence on this Planet.

Zahor...Remember • paper, weaving, wood, handmade paper • 1997

Sue Abbe Kaplan

I established Shulamis Press in the fall of 1996 with the intention of bringing to print works that explore Jewish themes in limited editions using traditional fine press production methods, hand-set metal type, a Vandercook cylinder press.

We Were Innocent: Eight Vignettes by Edzia J. Goldstein • letterpress with handset metal type, ed. 150 • original cyanotype (cover) by Marcia Brown • Shulamis Press • 1997

Tatana Kellner

In my work I deal with issues that personally touch my everyday life. These include: living in a rural environment; being a woman and an immigrant; reaching maturity; the death of friends and family members; the joy of being alive; and the frustrations of living in less than a perfect society.

As a daughter of Holocaust survivors born the generation after the war, I share survivor's guilt, anger and acceptance over the collective loss of those murdered. As an artist, I try to use these experiences and transform them into a contemporary context.

I began thinking about my experiences growing up in Czechoslovakia. Even though I have always known that my parents were interned in concentration camps and that both of their families were annihilated there, we never talked about those years in any detail. Those experiences indelibly changed my parents' outlook on life and in turn affected what they taught me about the world. Even though I grew up watching war movies, it wasn't until my adulthood when I read accounts of other Holocaust survivors that I realized how little I really knew of what actually happened to my family. I wanted to know more. Once I realized how I'd like to present my parents' stories, I asked them to recollect what happened, not only for myself, but also as evidence against the revisionists who claim the Holocaust never happened. Adding to the collective memory seemed especially important in light of the recurring incidents of anti-Semitism, racism, and ethnic cleansing we are witnessing.

The result of this search were two artists' books: *71125: Fifty Years of Silence* and *B-11226: Fifty Years of Silence*, where my parents document their nightmarish years in the concentration camps. In the course of working on these books I traveled to some of the concentration camp sites in order to understand what my parents were describing. This was an emotionally and psychologically wrenching experience. Actually standing in Auschwitz, I was finally able to visualize what actually happened there. Even

B-11226: Fifty Years of Silence · silkscreen, cast handmade paper · 1992

after 50 years with the patina of age, the horror was palpable. I photographed the camp sites as they are today and used these images in the books. I became so immersed in this subject that after the books were completed, I continued to create an entire body of large scale altered photographs recording the haunting memories these sites evoked which I hope will stand as a memorial to the Holocaust.

This extended project has directed my thinking about my Jewish heritage. Growing up in communist Czechoslovakia, religion of any kind was frowned upon, but the remnants of Hitler's propaganda made any practice of Judaism impossible.. My parents did not want me to be scarred as they were by the "accident of birth." When we came to the US we were sponsored by Jewish Family Services in Toledo, Ohio, and it was there that I first met Jews who were not afraid to acknowledge their heritage. While I am not a practicing Jew, the impact of the Holocaust on my life has deeply defined my work and thinking.

Not shown: *71125: Fifty Years of Silence* · 1992.

Judith Kerman

After almost 50 years of life as a secular Jew with spiritual yearnings, I have found communities within religious Judaism where I can explore the tradition in a way that works for me. My poems and bookworks are part of this exploration. While I have been a poet all my life, I feel a strong connection between my recent plunge into physical artmaking (much of it Judaica) and my explorations of the Jewish religious heritage. Bookworks are a natural meeting point for my artmaking and my poetry, and also another way to explore the Jewish heritage of engagement with the written word presented as part of special physical objects.

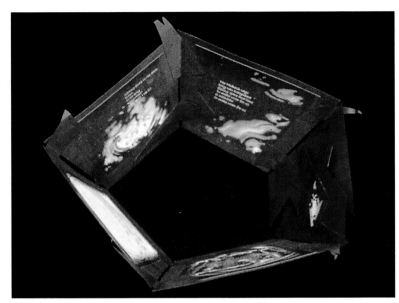

Vessels · paper structure with computer graphics, inkjet printer · 1997

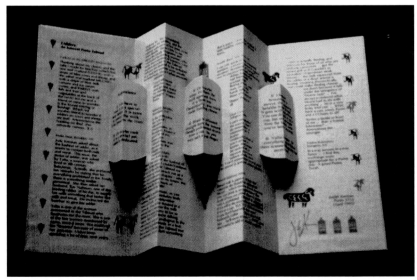

Udder Ambivalence · accordion pop-up with hand-cut rubber-stamp elements, scanned and printed on inkjet printer · 1997

Karen Klein

Deutscher · wood, acrylic, stain, rope · 1994

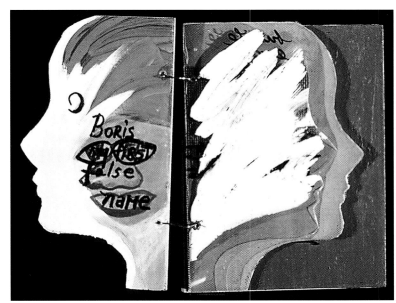

Federman · glass, wire, ink, mesh, acetate, acrylic · 1991

Although these Torah scrolls so central to Jewish experience speak about women, women are not authors of these texts. This places me as a woman in a mediated relationship to these text the described, but not a describer—someone whose story gets told, not someone who tells it. As a woman, then, making books myself connects me with this rich, traditional heritage, but on my own terms. For example, some of my books deal with the threat to Jewish survival and the persistence of that survival despite overwhelming odds. This theme is large and general, but my take on it emphasizes the irony, humor, and joy of that survival. As an artist who loves working with different materials, I find a place in the Jewish tradition of handwritten texts and the beautiful materials used to enclose them.

Lisa Kokin

Every time I take my x-acto blade to the tender page of a book I see my long-deceased grandfather's face before me. He is not happy. I am committing the Jewish equivalent of a mortal sin and believe me, I feel guilty. So powerful is my drive to rearrange and juxtapose, however, that I am willing to risk the wrath of my ancestors to accomplish my mission.

There's something about the silence and the intimacy of a book that lets me reveal things about myself that I wouldn't divulge if I were working in another form. Call it denial, but the fact is that if I put it between two covers, no secret is too private. Shy by nature, I like the medium of written word and

Six Books · Hebrew books, cow gut, acrylic · 1996
Courtesy: Catharine Clark Gallery, San Francisco

Babes in Goyland · mixed media, found photos, text, collection box · 1996
Courtesy: Catharine Clark Gallery, San Francisco

image and the intimacy between reader and artist it creates.

My definition of "book" is open-ended, a freedom which is many ways attributable to my lack of book art training. I am blissfully unaware of all the rules I am breaking as I go about my routine of sewing, stapling, riveting, and otherwise reconstituting objects to transform them into something readable. I use anything I can get my hands on, from toasters to minipads, as long as it isn't alive and squirming. I try to come up with something new every time so that each piece looks different from the last. Maybe then my grandfather, who gave me my first paint-by-number set, will forgive me.

48

Elaine Langerman

I wish to create realms of enchantment for the heart where it might find play and adventure. My wish is to coax the mind to give way to the spirit so that it may perceive and create in new ways, so that it might escape the illusion of limitation. Ah, to dance, to evolve through contemplation and joy!

Sefer · acrylic, pen, custom-made clamshell box · 1997

The Song of Songs · handmade paper, illumination with cover of wood, metal, ribbon, stones · 1997

Stephanie B. Later

*T*he *Song of Songs*, attributed to Solomon, has always been a source of dispute and mystery. Even the reference to Solomon in the title is questionable. Was Solomon the author of the work or was he the hero? Some researchers believe that the name "Solomon" was added perhaps only to give the work authority.

Although commonly accepted as sexual, its interpretation has always been disputed by clergy and scholars alike. However, the three most accepted interpretations are allegorical, dramatic, and anthological. Interpretations will always be challenged and the original concept may remain forever obscure, but in spite of all disputations, *The Song of Songs* is clearly dedicated to the exaltation of love and in my interpretation, man and woman's impassioned commitment to one another both spiritually and erotically.

Stephanie Brody Lederman

My grandmother had three sisters and three brothers, and they were born in Lodz, Poland. Before World War II, each sister was married and lived in the country of her husband, i.e. England, Belgium, and Germany. My grandmother came to New York City with her Polish-born husband (my grandfather); the brothers stayed in Poland. After the war, most of my relatives were presumed dead. Because I survived World War II due to the luck of being born in the USA, I feel an obligation to make my life worthwhile. I do this as an artist who tells stories with my heart, an artist who exposes the truth. This book contains photos (Xeroxed) of my German and Belgian relatives. The two little girls on the right were from Belgium, my second cousins. I would stare at this picture in my grandmother's chifrobe (chest of drawers). When questioned about them, my grandmother always answered, "Don't ask."

Grandma's War Pictures · collage, acrylic · 1996

An Artist in the University Medical Center · offset · 1989

May H. Lesser

The drawings, paintings and colored etchings which attend my reports and self-reflections celebrating life inside Tulane Medical School during the late 1980s reflects my knowledge of art history. I report on what I see both visually and verbally in this book. I see how physicians are trained to set aside their feelings and be scientific, so that they bury them. But this series allows them to re-feel these emotions at a safer time. I am interested in showing the intimacy and compassion between the doctor and his or her patient.

Paula Levine

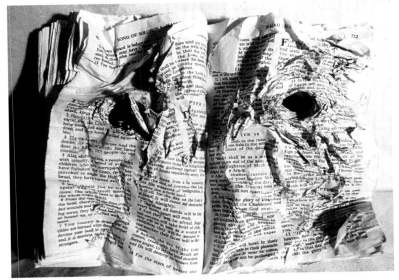

Scratched and Probed · The Bible · 1994

Hirsute · The Bible · 1992

The series called *as if the laws were malleable* contains more than 60 works of art, all using the Bible as both subject and object. Each of the pieces in the series stands as the evidence of a dialogue on matters of Judaism, convention and everyday life. Each bookwork is formed through systematic actions such as shrouding, wrapping, soaking and wringing dry, drilling, blending, rubbing, rending; these actions are intended to open up the text and reveal something of what metaphorically and symbolically lies beneath and within.

Each piece seeks to investigate, narrate from, and navigate along the fine line between law and awe.

Liliane Lijn (England)

Her *Mother's Voice* is the first volume in an auto-biographical trilogy, for which I interviewed my mother, asking her to tell me of her life and memories of her parents and grandparents. The result is an oral history presented on the fragile and tactile medium of rice paper thus mirroring the fragility of human life in general and in particular the fragility of a Jewish woman who lived through the panic years preceding the Second World War.

This book is particularly about being a Jewish woman in the 20th century, essentially about the restlessness of the rootless, those without home or land, those who have lost everything, even and most painfully their very past. In it I am letting my mother speak and although she speaks about the vicissitudes of her own life, she is also the mother I hold inside.

Her Mother's Voice · laser printed on Japanese papers, silver thread · 1996

Jenni Lukac

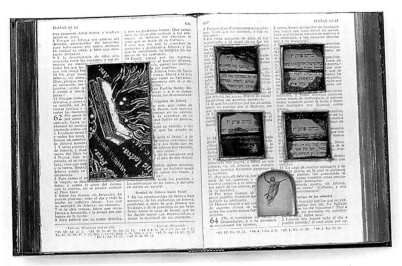

The Book of Isaiah · mixed media, paper, gold leaf, cyanotype print, ink, wax, glass · 1992

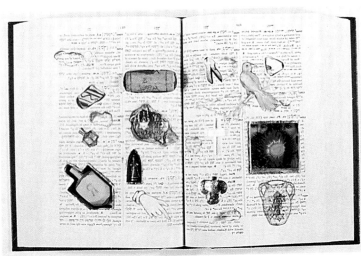

Kavannot · paper, mixed media with found objects · 1993

For five hundred years Jews secretly practiced their religion in the remote countryside of Portugal. Only recently have these communities practiced their Judaism openly, establishing congregations and synagogues and importing rabbis from Israel. As possession of Jewish books and holy objects was forbidden in Portugal from the time of The Inquisition, religious practice evolved into a syncretic form, incorporating folk culture and aspects of Christian iconography. The books I have created reflect these syncretic practices and beliefs, their Jewish aspects literally hidden within the physical structure of the books themselves. Objects include fragments found on the streets of the former Jewish quarters of several Portuguese towns, a dreidel found for sale at a local market in the north of Portugal, and fragments of dismembered religious books found in the basement of a family home in the U.S.

Joan Lyons

My Mother's Book · photo offset · 1982

Bible for a New World · 1897 Grimm-Webster German-English dictionary, altered, fusion and binding materials · 1997

Barbara Magnus

As a child I was told that to be Jewish was to be a good person and to make the world a better place. Being Jewish to me is about continuity. It is a way of being and a way of thinking about the world. It is being simultaneously open and skeptical, grateful and wary. It means never losing sight of the suffering in the world and never forgetting what it means to be uprooted and an immigrant with an abbreviated family tree. Being Jewish is to know or to find what is right and to amend what is not. It is the courage to do so in the face of adversity, and it is respect for diversity. Being Jewish is about seeing beneath the surface of the letter.

Judith Cohen Margolis (Israel)

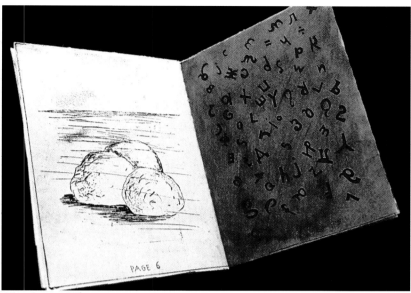

Abundance of Time • etching, cut and folded on Rives paper, hand painted with gouache • 1996

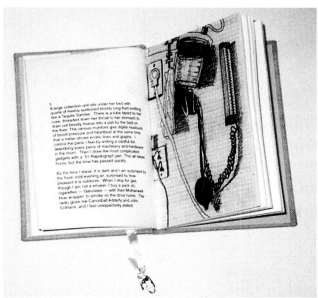

Life Support • laserprinted, handbound, silver amulet • 2000

Abundance of Time comes from the fact that the night before he died, my father sat up chatting with the night nurse at the hospital where he had checked in "just for tests." He spoke at length, she reported, about my mother, his children and grandchildren, his work, the trips he'd taken, and ended the conversation with "I've led a long and happy life and I've done everything I wanted to do." Then he went to sleep and died gently during the night.

And so the book images, with few or no words, are arranged in a sequence that allows the viewer to ponder this lovely legacy, and to imagine his or her own story in which there might be an abundance of time in which to do everything one wants.

Bubby · etching, text, found objects, fibers · 1997

Kathi Martin

Since I am not a religious Jew but have had a strong Jewish upbringing, I felt that my connection with Yiddish and with my Grandmother, Eva Michelson, was the most appropriate and sincere Jewish statement that I could make. I grew up going to Temple activities several times a week—social groups, summer camp, and my cousin Morton Bauman was Rabbi at Temple Beth Hillel for many years. My relationship with my Grandmother epitomizes the richness of this experience.

OCTOBER 5, 1939. FROM OUR WINDOW
I WATCHED THE VICTORIOUS NAZI
TROOPS PARADE THROUGH WARSAW.
THE GERMANS LOOKED INVINCIBLE.

Warsaw · linocuts · 1996
Previously published in *Light in the Shadows*, by Barbara Milman
(Jonathan David Publishers, Inc. http://www.jdbooks.com)

Barbara Milman

In 1994 I decided to interview Holocaust survivors and make a series of linocuts based on their stories. Because of the passage of time, a day will come when there are no more witnesses of the Holocaust to talk to us, when all we have will be some photographs, memoirs, and records of interviews. But there are still survivors willing to tell their stories. Over the course of two years, five such individuals agreed to be interviewed by me for these prints. I made a set of 12 prints for each person's story.

Not shown: *Light in the Shadows* · 1997.

Beverly Naidus

My cultural background (it was never religious) is both a large and small part of who I am as a person and as an artist. I fear being ghettoized by this part of my identity, particularly because I am so uninformed about Jewish religious practices and traditions. My spiritual identity is not so easily labeled and has almost nothing to do with Judaism (the big exception is my love of liberation seders). But I am proud of my cultural heritage. The burdens of its history, the *yiddishkeit* humor and wisdom, the questioning (often considered "troublemaking"/wandering; how many more times am I going to be moving in this lifetime?/nurturing; I don't think we made enough food) stereotypes are deeply a part of who I am.

What Kind of Name is That? · laminated laser prints, spiral bound · 1996

Miriam Neiger (Israel)

These "books" are "emotional objects." In each pair of pages there is a documentation in shapes, color, and sometimes in words of consciousness, emotion, and spiritual energy. Therefore they might also be called "diaries." Since each pair of pages was composed on a different day, impressions of inner events, which can be very distinct from each other, are included in the diaries.

As a member of the "second generation of the Holocaust" and as an Israeli, I would emphasize the concept of survival as an important issue in my life and creative work. And as part of the "People of the Book," I love books. I am afraid they will disappear in this computerized world. I create books, paint them, and copy texts in handwriting. In a way I return to the times when the book's creator and the artist's hand had direct physical contact with the magic of letters, shapes, and colors, whether it was put on paper, parchment, or papyrus.

Land of Milk and Honey · mixed media, ink on paper · 1996

How to Turn the Pages of a Burning Book · installation · 1997

Wendy Oberlander (Canada)

Over the past ten years, I have created a body of work composed of temporary installations, punctuated by other projects. Looking back, I see these as one larger, on-going project: that of revealing the hidden. I don't aim to erase it—I only wish to see it, articulate it, oftentimes touch it. The narrative shifts, the medium shifts but the questions remain. This is what compels me.

In turn, these questions are nurtured by books. It is too simple to add the words "question" and "book" together and see a reason revealed: because I am a Jew. But, indeed, all of the above is true. Questions and books are my inheritance, but not because I am Jewish. The world is far more complex than this, and I am a sum of many diverse parts and experiences. At the best of times, I hope that my work is a box full of riddles in a state of flux and transformation, with a little humor thrown in for good measure.

Laurel Paley

Jews love and worship a sacred text, each one studying, arguing, and participating in the creation of meaning. In my work, a layered language of symbol, texture, gesture and hierarchy, both open and veiled, also begs multiple interpretations, interpretations that change over time.

For me, being both an artist and a Jew are linked. Both groups tangibly express their principles and world views, the Jew through right action (*mitzvot*) and the artist through visual representation. And both groups see themselves as apart from society [she-lo-asanu k'goyel ha'aratsot—(G-d) didn't make us like the world's other people] while seeking to engage and affect the world from which they are "separate."

According to tradition, all Jews must write out the Torah for themselves. My work is that Sefer Torah, a sacred, ongoing conversation about what it means to be human.

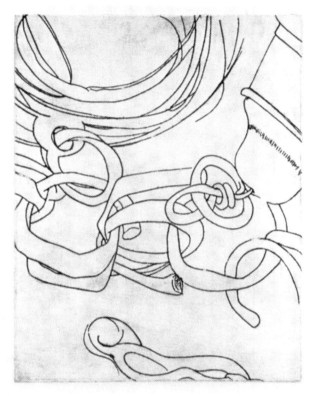

Links · intaglio, etching, aquatint, spit bite, sugarlift · 1992

Io Palmer

I was born to an African American father and a Jewish mother twenty-seven years ago in Greece. I have been blessed with an outstanding, eclectic, and colorful family who have been an endless source of creative inspiration. I began a series of clay books to give homage to them.

Ruth is one of the great Aunts on my mother's side of the family. She is famous for her ability to sell anything to anyone. My mother would tell me "You could go into a store wanting to buy a lamp and leave with a couch." She was always good at making me laugh; I was often doubled over in pain listening to her. Blue plaid is her favorite pattern, and she wears it often along with lots of heavy gold jewelry. She is compact and stable and not quite understated. This book is a small way of my paying tribute to a wonderful person.

Aunt Ruth · clay · 1997

Vaughan Rachel

My parents were marginally observant Christians and culturally I grew up in an Irish Catholic/Anglo Saxon Episcopalian household. When I married Allan Kaprow in 1955, I wanted to convert to Judaism and I chose Rachel as my Hebrew name. Due to a tragedy in my family, I found it difficult to hide deep grief. I began a long period of self repair by studying the Mishnah, I went to Israel as a Volunteer for Israel in the Israel Defense Forces, and I studied meditation. These books reflect how my being Jewish has everthing to do with my life and my art: there is no separation.

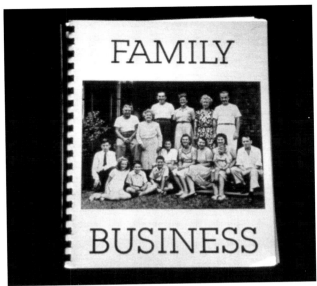

Family Business · photo offset, spiral bound · 1981

1975 Feminist Seder · 13 black and white photos, color Xeroxed with text · 1999

Sonya Rapoport

The *Transgenic Bagel* is a parody on a gene-splicing theme. The state-of-the-art bagel technology allows the reader-consumer to alter personality upon eating a recombinant bagel. The gene-splicing theme is based on the assumption that Noah's Ark comprised the first gene pool. Each animal that resided in this virtual ark had the character trait associated with a Biblical personality from the Book of Genesis. As an adolescent Jewish girl, I wished to repress those Biblical traits so I could be accepted into my Boston WASP environment. Here, the reader can decide to select the opposite of these Jewish trait genes in order to conform to a WASP personality.

The Transgenic Bagel · laser printed · 1997

Eva-Lynn Ratoff

Morning Prayers · rice papers, handmade papers, acrylic, ink, watercolor, pencils · 1997

Sh'ma · handmade papers, inks, watercolor, pencils, acrylic · 1997

Judaism plays a vital role in my life and work. Inspired by Torah, prayers, songs and images, my work expresses my feelings about Judaism. There is an inner need for me to relate our joys and sadnesses and especially the hope for peace. With words and color, my art reflects my soul. It is my hope to bring to others moments of spirituality and to remind them what it is to be a Jew.

Gail S. Rebhan

In "Mother-Son Talk," I playfully explore the development of cultural identity and stereotypes in my young sons. I use color photographs that I have taken, along with images from newspapers, postcards, books, advertising, television, computer games, and old black and white photographs.

I am exploring issues of identity and stereotypes, including religious identity in my art. Before I had children I would have described myself as a secular Jew. When my older son was about four, I realized that if I wanted my kids to grow up with a sense of Jewish identity I had to become more observant. This year my older son is having a bar mitzvah. He has gone from ambivalence about being Jewish to accepting his faith and Jewish identity. My younger son never questioned his religious identity. My work explores these and other cultural and social issues.

Mother–Son Talk · offset · 1996

Remember Babi Yar · mixed media · 1997

Marilyn R. Rosenberg

I am a Jew. It was twelve days before my 7th birthday, and if my grandparents had not left Russia at the turn of the century, I could have been there, grown up there, died there, near Kiev at Babi Yar, on September 29 or 30, 1941. As I become the older generation, less and less of us remember those war years. So, I remember, I feel I must tell about the Holocaust. I cannot forget, ever.

Sophia Rosenberg

(Canada)

Lilith Scroll · handmade paper, photographs, acetate · 1994

This piece began an investigation into the Biblical first woman Lilith (who, as it turns out, is likely the remnant of an earlier middle eastern Goddess). She had been appearing in my dreams and I kept stumbling across references to her. She seemed to embody all the things that had been exiled or edited out of religious Judaism: the feminine, the sexual, the psychic, the mystical, the dark. An aura of fear surrounded her and a wealth of amulets was designed to keep her away. *Who was she?*

Biblically she was the woman created with Adam, the two together being made in the image of G-d. She refused to lie beneath him and fled the garden to take residence beside the Red Sea where she is said to have given birth to demons. She is blamed for infant death and wet dreams. *Uncontrollable—connected to sex and birth and death.*

I began to explore her in myself, costuming myself and letting her dance. On one of these occasions, Catherine took the photographs in this piece. The poems, too, are my written remnants of this exploration.

The form of the scroll carries obvious allusions to the Torah and all that is sacred to Jews. By creating a scroll to Lilith, I was, in a sense, making a space for her (and for the dark, female, sexual, mystic part of myself). I was reclaiming some of the power behind the taboos regarding women, blood, sexuality, and death.

The piece, itself, was done in collaboration. Catherine Gilchrist's beautiful photos acted as the impetus to make the poems into a book. Deborah Hodgkinson (paper/bookmaker extraordinaire) and Catherine and I cut and pasted together late into the night (and nearly set fire to Deb's paper store). The Goddess was with us.

Marleene Rubenstein

In the Yizkor series, I explore the excavation of memory by researching family history to create a visual regeneration of relatives murdered in the Nazi Holocaust fifty years ago. The visual manifestation of this investigative process is that most ancient of Jewish memorial media—the book. The metaphor of loss becomes a slippage from the original referent so that the books become an auratic object within their own right, referencing specific individuals but retaining their own particularized identity. In several of the pieces, an appropriated book is altered physically and conceptually to metamorphose into a new work. The transformed piece becomes an intervention, a receptacle for defacement or erasure of some kind to reiterate historical events through the creative process itself. The act of creating the manifestation of absence becomes ritualized into an act of mourning.

Passage · Xerox, handmade paper, cotton thread · 1997

Linda Rubinstein

I was raised as a Jew and I became a painter, seemingly unrelated events. Yet as I grew older and began to make books, and as my books became the work of reflection, I found Judaism to be at times a thread and other times the fabric of my work. My books are about the experiences of a Jewish woman, artist, curator, wife, mother, in late 20th century America.

The questions my books often ask - Who am I? What has shaped me? Where am I going in life? What do I stand for? - are truly ancient questions. And although I do not seek purely Jewish answers, my reflections are shaped by my immediate history and by several thousand years of Jewish history to which I am connected.

Not shown: *Two Lives* · 2000.

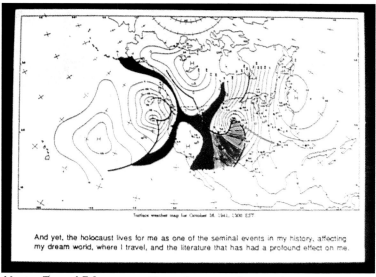

And yet, the holocaust lives for me as one of the seminal events in my history, affecting my dream world, where I travel, and the literature that has had a profound effect on me.

Moving Toward Fifty · paper, Xeroxed images, color pencil · 1993

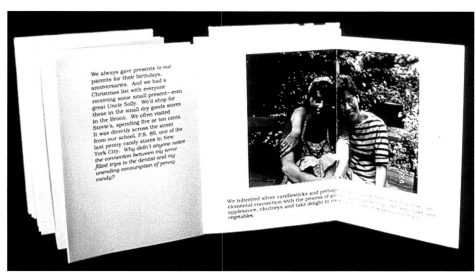

The Judy / Linda Book · color Xeroxed photos, laser printed · 2000

Diaspora Menorah • copper, bronze and paper • 1995

Rochelle Rubinstein (Canada)

Everything that I create, as an artist and a Jew, caught between different systems of belief and culture, is an attempt to reconcile and repair. I use my circumscribed vocabulary of images to play with my own repression; with my legacy as a daughter of religious Holocaust survivors; with memory, its contortions and displacements; with desire and the transcendent self.

I have handwritten the traditional text, a lament for Jerusalem and Judea after the siege and destruction by the Babylonians in 586 BCE, and added my rubber stamped images. I am trying to associate the images intimately with language, turning word toward icon and icon toward word. I have taken some liberties with the English text (but not with the Hebrew...), mainly by shifting the focus from resignation to G-d's will, confessions, and prayers, to struggles in female-male relationships. The imagery serves as commentary on and counterpoint to the texts.

Book of Lamentations/Echah • handwritten text, hand colored rubber stamps and photos of photoblock prints on fabric, felt cover • 1996

Alyssa C. Salomon

One of the issues with which I have dealt in my work is the paradox within modern Jewish identity of the Victim/Aggressor and the inherent instability of this dichotomy. The menorah—a flammable one—has been for me a way to embody this paradox. The Menorah is essential in the celebration of Chanukah, which has evolved into a major holiday and been made to symbolize a miracle of military skill and will. This piece, *Diaspora Menorah*, is portable, pocket-sized, utilitarian and functional. Small, made of inexpensive metal, these menorahs folded away in luggage to be opened in hotel rooms by traveling salesmen and the like away from home during Chanukah.

Jews—a people dispersed throughout the world—carry their beliefs, customs, and metaphors with them as they wander and as they journey. Ceremonies and ceremonial objects serve as touchstones for practice and identity. Every Jew learns to light candles. Every Jewish home includes a menorah. Because this menorah is constructed of paper in addition to metal, the menorah is flammable. There is risk in its use. I equate this danger of fire with the dangers inherent in the imagery of military strength celebrated by the Jewish Community today.

Robyn Sassen (South Africa)

This transmogrified passport is an official South African passport and deals with the issues raised in terms of the realization of a home land and the unavoidable problems present in identifying people in terms of caste, country of origin or race. I have used various means of transposing text onto the pages in this passport, and have dipped the entire work into beeswax.

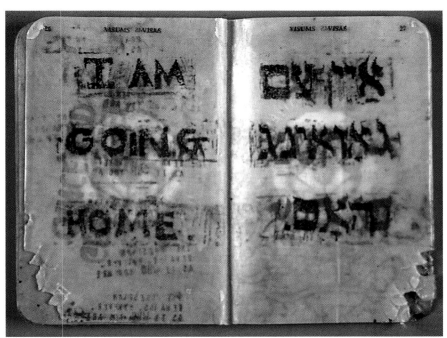

Identity Text · South African Identity Document, beeswax, stamps, and mixed media · 1997

Claire Jeanine Satin

Q/ZZ Bookwork/Catalog • power-coated metal mesh, printed acetate, fiberglass screen, 4 inserted books, braided wire, plastic power-coated aluminum screen • 1997

JCMCJJ/Dancers on a Plane/Bookwork VI • steel, braided wire, brass filings, metallic pigments, handwritten reassembled text • 1997

Miriam Schaer

Eve's Meditation • acrylic, ink, Xerox, beads, colored pencil, silk • 1997

My books tend to be kinetic sculptures created with papers, fabrics, beads, and objects. In *Eve's Meditation* these take the form of a serpent, a book and a fruit, the shape of which fills the serpent with the spirit of hidden knowledge. The path to knowing, therefore, is through the belly of the snake.

More than this, it suggests that knowledge is dangerous and apart, allied with temptation, acquired in disobedience, and punished by shame—all signs of the significance of the outsider, the guest denied the feast, and characteristic of my own relationship to Judaism. Growing up Jewish in western New York State, my earliest memories are of apartness. Yet our apartness created a lasting current that makes it difficult for me to accept a story at face value. To find the story in the story, to tease out the text between the lines, sensing so often that all is in the not said, I find myself still applying the legacy of an outsider looking in, shaped like *Eve's Meditation* by an outward assimilation that leaves me still Jewish at the core.

Helen Schamroth

(New Zealand)

I was born in Poland in 1945—my father had escaped from a concentration camp, and my mother had lived on her wits and false papers. They were two solitary people who had lost everyone. We left Europe in 1949 and moved to Australia, to lead a "normal life."

Being an adult Jew in a small community in Auckland was different from identifying with the larger Jewish community in Melbourne where I grew

Out of the Darkness · paper, cotton, computer-generated, photo-copied images and text on acetate · 1994

New World Old Story · inkjet digital images, acetate, paper, cardboard, foamboard, aluminum · 1997   Collaborator: Michael Smythe

up. I realize now that I used to keep my head down and try to merge with the mainstream community. My Jewishness was not hidden, but was nonetheless fairly private, kept within the home and Jewish circles.

I reached middle age before I stepped over the line and started producing art that was overtly Jewish. Perhaps it was because I discovered mortality of my parent and friends; perhaps I grew up; perhaps the support of a small Jewish feminist group gave me strength.

Now I find that my Jewishness is my starting point in my art, and it is there for the world to see. My works are often symbolic, a personal/political journey. They are about my Jewish heritage, my environment, and about being a woman.

Arleen Schloss

My work with letters and language is a celebration of life and my Jewish heritage.

Funny, you don't look ish · paper, color Xerox · 1997

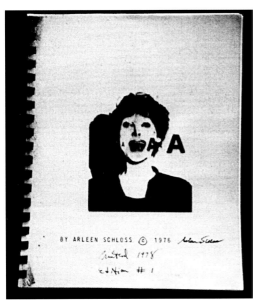

A Book, ed. #1 · black and white xerography · 1978

Mira Schor

Writing as a visual image has been an important part of my visual art work off and on since the mid-seventies. Diaristic text was the subject of early works. Appropriation from the language of politics, the judiciary and military spheres of public lives formed the core of my work from the late eighties and early nineties, and, since 1994, language is used as a self-referential sign. I try to embed the gap between visual and verbal languages within each other materiality and meaning.

The visualization of text was at the core of my parents' art work. My parents, Ilya and Resia Schor, made jewelry and objects of Judaica, as well as paintings. Of consistent interest to me are their silver and gold mezuzahs: not only did they engrave and delineate Hebrew letters on each mezuzah—letters that I could *only* appreciate as images, because I do not read Hebrew—but also I was fascinated and influenced by the knowledge that an unseen talismanic text was secreted inside these small sculptured treasures.

In *Funny, You Don't Look ish*, the word *jewish* is never fully spelled out, to reflect that G-d cannot be named and to parallel the injunction against graven images. It is deferred and referred to, through individual letters, onomatopoeic language bits, and the repetition of the word fragment *ish*, as in the *Yellow Submarine* line, "Funny, you don't look blueish."

Judith Serebrin

Books have played a significant role in my life. They have given me hope and insight, refuge and delight. I grew up in Salt Lake City, Utah where there were not many Jews. I felt a great sense of isolation. What impressed me was the value of the written word, of books and storytelling in Jewish culture. These things were my primary connection to the Jewish world. In particular, the scrolls of the Torah and Megillah (The Book of Esther) were objects that fascinated me from an early age.

Having been away from Utah for some time, I now create packages of bound images to be contemplated. I strive to create glimpses into my present, past, and future. Books have become a way of exploring my relationships to Judaism and Jewish culture, to G-d and feminism, to family and liberation. I choose images, words, and materials which capture or allude to different and sometimes conflicting aspects of these relationships. Similar to the ritual tying of the *tephillin*, binding these diverse elements together into books and scrolls allows me to meditate and struggle with these complex relationships.

Pain & Punishment (taking a look at Eve & how, as Jewish women, we associate pain with punishment) · scroll, mixed media · 1997

Joyce Cutler Shaw

The Stones of Dachau · cotton image pages, vellum text pages, magnesium covers · 1997

The *Stones of Dachau* represents part of an extended visual and poetic odyssey of parallel paths. One is a journey in search of the world's first bird, which traces the seven scattered fossils of the archaeopteryx, all discovered in neighboring limestone quarries in Bavaria. These are famous and rare examples of a transitional form which bears visible evidence of its own evolution from reptile into bird. With scales, a tail and teeth, with claws along its wings, and with feathers, it catches evolution in the act. The second is a journey, or pilgrimage, to World War II Holocaust sites, which include Dachau in Bavaria. The stones were discovered in elongated, parallel rows, which marked the former sites of barracks for interned prisoners. Connecting nature and human nature, this continuing odyssey is a quest for signs of our own evolution from mammal to human to humane.

Karen Shaw

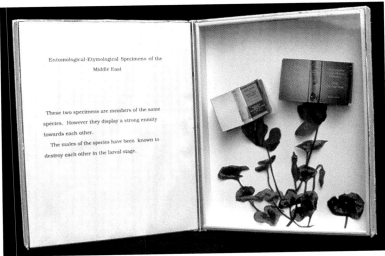

Etymological/Entomological Specimens · mixed media · 1993

Market Research · offset · 1978

I was born into a very secular Jewish household in the Bronx, New York City, so it is difficult for me to define what being Jewish means to me other than a cultural, psychological, and sociological milieu. Perhaps because we are called "People of the Book," I make books. Even though some of my work alludes to the cabalistic system of Gematria, I came upon the number/language system from a job as a statistician working on a survey for NBC and from being a person sensitive to the numerous complexities of 20th century life whereby numbers trail us in every endeavor.

Not shown: *Less is More.*

Genie Shenk

Bias · photocopy, laser prints, collage, mixed media · 1997

Bias is about a time of pivotal confrontation with the set of oddly abstract prejudices I acquired as a child. Social, religious, racial, and economic attitudes had reached me quietly, mostly through whisper, nuance, innuendo, common practice. They were absorbed as if by osmosis, prejudices that existed largely as caveats on a hypothetical level, without explanation and with no experiential grounding whatever—we lived in homogeneous parts of the South and my schoolmates were all practically identical. A move to New Orleans when I was in Junior High provided a context, a theater, where I saw the things I'd learned play out. New Orleans had atmosphere and I loved it; compared to everywhere else we had been, it was colorful and exciting. It was also diverse. Having changed schools frequently, I was all too familiar with the insecurity of being new, but in this densely Catholic city, I was for the first time a member of another kind of minority, somewhat excluded, very much left out. I'd always been a watcher, and as I encountered different kinds of people, started to question and to feel. What was it, really, to be Catholic? Protestant? Jewish? black? divorced? Couldn't they see how they were hurting each other? Judgments had come to life and taken on faces—faces I liked, faces like mine, my own face.

As I worked on *Bias*, I began to realize it was an homage to my mother. Many of its images turned up when I had the sad duty last year of emptying out her house and found consolation in things saved carefully from earlier, happier times. She had loved the city, it had freed her, and though she moved away, she never really left. She had tried hard to do her duty and raise me as a proper Southern belle, but that didn't take, and I like to think it was her underlying better sense that really taught me.

Elena Mary Siff

Having to think about my lack of Jewish identity in regard to the creation of this "book object" has been a personal journey for me, a journey of profound significance which has put me in touch with my long-departed grandparents and their three sons, one of whom was my fascinating father, Philip, who basically ignored his Jewish identity for all of my life with him. He wanted me to learn about my Jewish half because he kept every letter, document, article, etc. about his early life that I knew little about. He must have known that I would find these clues when he died in 1981—on my birthday—and that I would connect the strands of these lives to my own. I learnt through these documents that there was great tragedy in my father's life and he never spoke of these things, because it caused him too much pain.

I never knew my Jewish paternal grandparents (my maternal grandparents were Italian) as my father's father died when my father was a young man. I only saw my grandmother Mary a few times when I was about 5 years old. Religion played no part in my upbringing and what I know about "being Jewish" has come from my husband and my Jewish friends.

My father loved to travel and every year until I was twelve years old, we lived in a different place, so I often felt "rootless," as did my grandfather, as did my father. This exhibition has compelled me to discover the difficult and troubled history of my Jewish half, and for this I am grateful.

Rootless: On the Road with my Jewish Self · old red metal truck, mixed media, old letters, documents, photographs · 1997

Suzanne Maura Silver

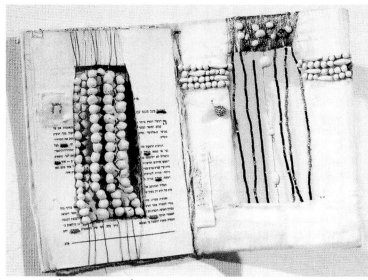

Haruzim (Rhymes/Beads) · mixed media · 1997

For several years my work has focused on language as a physical object, exploring it together with art and learning in an attempt to define cultural meaning. I use traditional signs and symbols associated with Judaism as well as more contemporary Judaic images. Through my work I investigate issues of cultural disposition: high versus low, religious versus secular, and cultural strength versus assimilation.

In the process of learning Hebrew, words and puns became sources of inspiration for a new series. This is represented by "Charuzim," work made from books (novels, technical manuals, guides) in which rhymes have been marked with beads, creating a new decorative object which venerates language, a secular alternative to the aesthetic traditions of the Psalter, the illuminated Bible, the hand-painted Haggadah, or the bejeweled Torah cover.

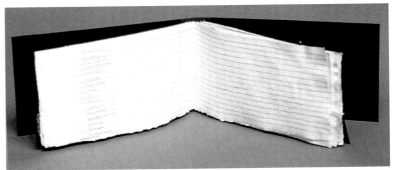

The Emperor's Clothes · cotton rag, abaca papers, human hair, gouache, ink, pins · 1997

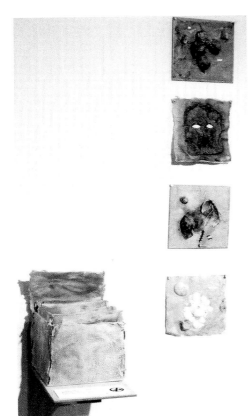

Morning Prayer · flax paper, stones, tea, human hair, gold filament thread, safety pins · 1997

Robbin Ami Silverberg

At its best, I am a member of the "People of the Book"…of a long and rich history of learning and thinking. At its worst, I am a descendant of a misogynist patriarchal people…one that I will repeatedly question and react against. Either way, it is a part of me and who I am. Many of my artist books have been identified as "Jewish" in theme; at the same time, being Jewish is not central to my work…being human is.

Jenny Snider

My parents spoke Yiddish to each other, but not to their children. As a result, the culture it represented seemed inaccessible. In 1977, while working on drawings for a film based on the Chelm stories, I began reading about the lives of Jews in the Eastern European shtetlakh. This research, and the drawings and paintings I subsequently made, led me to a new understanding, not only of Chelm, but of my own Jewish background.

I first loved the stories because of their outlandish imagery and self-critical humor. I came to love them more, because they led me to explore and identify with my own past. Most important, the Chelmites led me back to painting.

Chelmites are artists of a sort, searching for answers. Their search leads them to invent ladders to the moon and squander a fortune, filling the sky with feathers. Their harebrained solutions to mundane problems underscore a genius for rising above desperate conditions. I love these stories because they continue to yield metaphors. When I work, Chelm is alive and I am a resident.

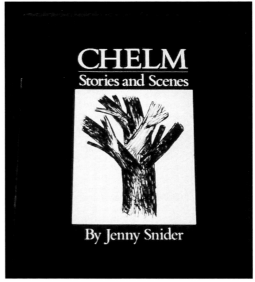

Chelm: Stories & Scenes · offset · 1978

Sefarim (Books) · cotton thread, wire · 1996

Franca Sonnino

(Italy)

Leah Sosewitz

After the birth of my son, I began to explore Judaic art with the creation of my sister's Ketubah. This exploration has continued to grow and expand, branching out into papercutting, illuminating, calligraphy, and bookmaking. My fascination with Judaic imagery and artforms and the endless possibilities which they hold for me contribute largely to my own personal sense of my Judaism. The interest which I have in Jewish ideas and texts has given me both inspiration for the making of art as well as a compass with which to navigate the world around me. Through words, images, and sound, I feel connected to the amazing history and survival of the Jewish people.

Jacob's Ladder · paper, collage, gold leaf · 1997

Victoria Stanton (Canada)

Fake Jewel · muslin, fabric, canvas, acetate, photos, photocopies, silkscreens, assorted jewelry, marker, thread, wood bar, screws · 1997

I have always known what my family's cultural heritage is (Jewish), but the combination of being brought up in a secular house, not having what are considered "typical" Jewish physical features (hence not "looking like a Jew"), and having a very non-Jewish sounding name, has always meant I could easily pass as a gentile. For years I considered this option desirable. I never questioned this ability to pass (indeed, I didn't know there was a name for it) and thought myself lucky. More recently, after reading such books as *The Issue is Power* (Melanie Kaye Kantrowitz) and questioning and discussing such issues as self-hatred, shame, re-connecting with one's cultural history, I have come to realize that there exists such internalized anti-Semitism and I have lived with it for most (if not all) of my life. I have questioned this "luck" at not inheriting "Jewish" features and begun to examine such notions as "looking like a Jew" (what on Earth does that mean? And what does it imply?). I've also begun to understand that physical appearance does not necessarily act as a measure of one's Jewishness and that I needn't try to hide behind my name anymore. This has led to uncovering my shame at being in-authentic, not being a "real" Jew but merely an imposter.

The process of creating the book, *Fake Jewel*, may serve to externalize and come to terms with this shame by allowing myself the opportunity to recognize it, to say it out loud, and to share it with others.

Ursula Sternberg

I always carry a sketchbook with me. I draw whatever I can. These books are visual diaries; they record people, places, events. Before starting a new book I decorate the cover, inside and out. Often I paint into the first few pages, by way of tuning up, for it is always difficult to begin a new book. Sometimes I invent a story for the painted page. In this way both words and image are closely connected without either being an illustration of the other.

Growing Up in Holland & Belgium · hand painted unique book, accordion · 1999

Carrie Ungerman

...*and a still small voice* uses the Bible I received for my Confirmation. I created a middle page on which I list all the women named in the Torah. The cut out letters of the aleph bet are inserted like book marks through the Bible. These letters, made out of Kosher parchment prepared specifically to be made into a Sefer Torah by a scribe, are the potential for the naming of all those women left un-named throughout the Torah, the foundation of Jewish life.

and a still small voice · Confirmation Bible, Kosher parchment, vellum, ink · 1998

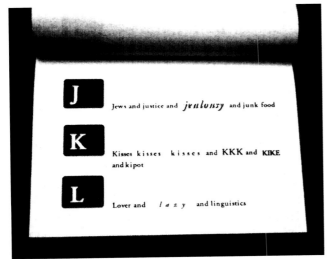

My Alphabet Book · computer generated on recycled paper with text, initial letters, illustration · 1997

Lila Wahrhaftig

My *Alphabet Book* was inspired by a family crisis. "Instead of eating or fighting with my husband, I decided to channel my feelings into an artwork, a free association alphabet book. Artists are supposed to be able to integrate their crises and emotions into their work; this is part of what being an artist is about. I also love my computer (something late middle-aged women aren't supposed to enjoy), and I really wanted to do something beautiful using computer technology. The book incorporates words that most women understand, words that may have a completely different meaning for men."

Ruth Wallen

Russian Lessons · mixed media, dye sublimation prints, paper, cloth, paint · 1997

As a child I loved to listen to my grandmother's stories. I imagined curling up with sisters above the stove to sleep or waiting alone in the forest after the horse came unhitched from the buggy she was driving. Equally fascinating were the bits and pieces of family gossip that I heard during our biannual pilgrimages to New York. Transported from the isolation of a California suburb, for a month or so I found myself in a dense web of relatives with more cousins and great aunts and uncles than I could possible keep track of.

More than anything else, what I remember from religious school is that every Jew must make his or her own interpretation of the Torah. As a Jew, I can identify as both insider and outsider. I am always looking for the other side of the story. I seek to clarify the moral or social implications of an argument. To be Jewish means to respect the power of words, to challenge rigid prejudices or simple thinking. I am aware that there is always another layer. The resonance between the stories is more significant than the truth of a single tale.

Ellen Wallenstein-Sea

To me, growing up Jewish meant having a name that was ethnic and recognizable. It meant that you could have been in a concentration camp. It meant an identification with a people and a culture. It meant summer camp and Friday night services, Hebrew prayers I know by rote but not by meaning. It meant holiday dinners, celebrations, and family.

Auschwitz Box · wooden box, paper, art reproduction, Hebrew prayer book pages, doll, felt, buttons, teeth, hair · 1997

Book of my Ancestors, 1985–86 · Xerox pages collaged with copies of original photographs, family photographs · 1985

Ruth Weisberg

Forgotten Faces Renamed · vellum, found objects, hydrus watercolor, photography · 1997
Courtesy: Jack Rutberg Fine Arts, Los Angeles

In Judaism, both remembering and naming are redemptive acts. Over a dozen years ago, I came upon a found photograph in my friend, Annie Shaver Crandell's loft in New York City. She had discovered it in some debris out on the street. For me the image of a classroom of Jewish girls was deeply moving. They were utterly familiar—I recognized them, yet I saw them across what seemed an unbridgeable chasm of time and history. Five years ago, I asked my friend to give me the photograph as I knew that some day I would use it as the point of departure for a work of art. *Forgotten Faces Renamed* is that piece.

Sabell Bender sat with me looking at the face of each girl as we discovered their names. Yes, that must be a Hinde, "don't you think she is an Itke and this other one is a Feygeleh." Then Sabell wrote each name in Yiddish and I wrote the accompanying transliteration of their beautiful Yiddish names. Malka, Nekhama, Sheyne, Hodl and Libbe…Zissl, Dovyzeh and Yehudis…forgotten faces have been renamed.

Gayle Wimmer

My father was a (gentle) tyrant. For 48 years I struggled against his imprint. Then he became terminally ill and his hard edges began to soften. Whether this was the effect of his illness, his medications, or a conscious decision is not clear. During those final two years he grew increasingly more philosophical, light-hearted, and receptive, and I recorded our talks in my journal. This work evolved from having borne witness to his transition from life to death. On each of the twelve cotton handkerchiefs which belonged to my father, the words in the text are his; the MRI brain images are mine.

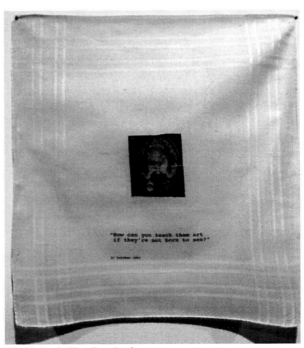

My Father's Handkerchiefs · 12 cotton handkerchiefs, Xerox transfer, printed · 1997

Biographies

Judith A. Hoffberg, *librarian and archivist, editor and publisher (Umbrella Editions), curator and art writer, has been involved with artist books for the past 35 years as a collector, curator, and critic. She has organized many exhibitions throughout the United States and has lectured on the subject throughout the world. She publishes a newsletter, Umbrella, which features news and reviews of artist books. She resides in Santa Monica, California.*

Ita Aber, a New York City artist, is a sculptor and textile artist, renowned throughout the United States for her work over the past fifty years. She has curated over fifty exhibits dealing with contemporary art, ancient art, textiles, Judaica, ethnography, sculpture, photography, etc. She has had many one person exhibitions from the 1970s through the 1990s, as well as participating in many museum group exhibitions. She is the author of *The Art of Judaic Needlework* (1979) and has installed many sculptures in Jewish institutions in the East Coast. In January 2001, she had a 55-year retrospective exhibition at New York Artists Equity Broome Street Gallery.

Joyce Abrams, a New York City artist, educated at Columbia University (MFA) and at Cooper Union (BFA), has exhibited widely throughout the New York City gallery scene with painting, drawing and mixed media. She has also curated exhibitions and is in many public and private collections. She is presently in Japan on a US-Japan Exchange grant to do research on her father, who was one of the first businessmen to enter Japan after World War II.

Melinda Smith Altshuler, based in Los Angeles, has a degree from California State University, Northridge. She has exhibited in many exhibitions, especially with her installations and works using found objects. As co-executive director of SITE, an artists' non-profit organization, she curated and moderated many events and exhibitions in the 1990s.

Lynne Avadenka is a professional calligrapher, and an instructor of Book Arts and Typography, having taught at Wayne State University and the University of Michigan. She is proprietor of Land Marks Press, which has produced limited edition books and broadsides, especially with Jewish themes. She has curated several exhibitions in Michigan, and received an NEA and a Creative Artist Grant from the Michigan Council for the Arts. Her bookworks have been included in many collections such as the Library of Congress, Israel Museum, New York Public Library, and others.

Beth Bachenheimer has an MFA from Vermont College in Montpellier, a BFA from California Institute of the Arts, and is Los Angeles-based. She is known for her mask making, but her bookwork in the exhibition documents the annihilation of her family during the Nazi era, except for her father who was saved and sent to the United States. She has appeared in countless exhibitions throughout California with her work on masks, paper, installations, and bookworks.

Marion A. Baker is known for her etchings, linocuts, and ceramic tiles. In 1978, she learned letterpress printing at the Women's Building in Los Angeles, and from that time she has made artist books on her own press. She has been educated at UC Berkeley and UCLA. She has had many solo shows, as well as having been invited to many exhibitions with her bookwork.

Susan Bee is the daughter of Jewish immigrants to the U.S, both parents being artists. She has a B.A. in art history and painting, and an M.A. in Creative Art from Hunter College. She has participated in many group shows since 1972 to the present, as well as having solo shows of her books and paintings at Granary Books in 1997, the Virginia Lust Gallery in New York in 1992, and at A.I.R. Gallery in 2000. Along with Mira Schor, she has also been co-editor, designer and publisher of *M/E/A/N/I/N/G*, a journal of contemporary art issues. *Little Orphan Anagram* was done in collaboration with her husband and longtime collaborator, Charles Bernstein, dealing with some of the dangers and pitfalls of innocence.

Miriam Beerman of Montclair, New Jersey, is the oldest artist in the show, a painter and printmaker for nearly 50 years. The past five years has involved the artist in making one-of-a-kind bookworks. Her book *Survival* includes drawings made in the spirit of automatism and chance, reflecting a sea of subconscious imagery with words by Jewish poets and writers, i.e. Primo Levi, Paul Celan, Rose Drachler, Adrienne Rich, Denise Levertov, Eugenia Ginzburg, Osip Mandelstam and others who constantly inspire her.

Lauren Berkowitz is one of the outstanding emerging artists of Australia, known for her installation art including bags, bottles, newspapers, or the collected histories of the neighborhood in which she lives, as well as homage to Rothko, Barnett Newman and Yves Klein. Educated both in Melbourne and New York City, she has begun a brilliant career with solo and group exhibitions, as well as critical recognition. She comes from a Polish family that immigrated to Australia because of World War II.

Gaza Bowen of Santa Cruz, California is a self-taught artist whose reputation for making art in the form of shoes has been renowned, but her own heritage appears in *The Secret Game*, a memory of being born Jewish in the South during World War II with the text evoking a secure, cheery American middle class. The book tells the story of playing in her best friend's attic their self-invented game of "Anne Frank." The bookwork speaks of the moment of encounter between two cultures.

Jo-Ann Brody is a graduate of Reed College and the Portland Museum Art School in Oregon. Brody, resident of Peekskill, New York, has been a ceramist for the past 30 years, creating female torsos and figures in clay. This, her first bookwork, celebrates her life and that of her daughter, a kind of Ketuba in clay. The book speaks of past, present, and future.

Rose Ann Chasman of Chicago, Illinois has been working in book arts for over 20 years including Hebrew calligraphy and the traditional folk-art of papercutting, pushing the boundaries of these crafts with innovative materials and techniques. The letters of the Hebrew alphabet, traditionally seen as G-d's first creation and used in mystic meditation, are an important element in her work. Although having received formal art training at Antioch College, University of Chicago, and the Art Institute of Chicago, her papercutting and calligraphic skills are self-taught. Her work in recent years has become simultaneously both larger and smaller, entirely hand-cut and hand-made.

Deborah Davidson, a resident of the Boston area, has been tracing her family whose roots go back to 1350. The family in Spain was expelled after the Inquisition and landed in Italy. The bookwork in this exhibition, *Voce*, is a response to her maternal great-grandmother's 8 letters written from an internment camp in Italy in 1944. She was killed at Auschwitz very soon after the last letter was written. Davidson's response to the political is the personal.

Abbe Don, president of Abbe Don Interactive, Inc., which she founded in 1994, is an interface designer and interactive multimedia artist, specializing in digital storytelling. She is best known for her innovative interactive family album *We Make Memories* which has been exhibited in the U.S. and Europe. As a student at Scripps College, she printed a book about her Bubbe (grandmother) entitled, *No Soup, Just Matzo Balls*, which has since been translated into an interactive family storytelling, *Bubbe's Back Porch,* which can be viewed and contributed to on the World Wide Web at <http://www.bubbe.com>. She resides in San Francisco, California.

Barbara Drucker of Santa Monica, California, a professor at the University of California, Los Angeles, has been involved in the making and exhibiting of artist books for many years. Born a Jew in New York, she has always been interested in all religions and all peoples. After going to Greece to experience the Greek Easter religious celebrations and rituals firsthand, she saw connections between psychology, religion and artmaking. Through subsequent trips to Greece, she learned more about Christianity, its current practice and the meaning it holds for a whole group of people, and thus more about its source, Judaism. She explores through her art the relationship to both sets of beliefs, feeling nurtured by and outside of both.

Johanna Drucker, artist, printer, publisher and writer, has been making artist books since 1972; as is indicated by her name, "Drucker," she is also a printer of her bookworks. After teaching at Columbia University, she became professor of Contemporary Art and Theory at Yale University in the Department of History of Art. She is the author of many publications including *The Visible Word* (University of Chicago Press, 1994), *Theorizing Modernism* (Columbia University Press, 1994), and the *Alphabetic Labyrinth* (Thames and Hudson, 1995); creative titles include *Narratology* (Druckwerk, 1994), *Otherspace: Martian Ty/opography* (Nexus Press, with Brad Freeman, 1993) and *Dark Decade* (Detour Press, 1995). She is the author of *The Century of Artists' Books* (New York, Granary Books, 1995). She presently holds the Robertson Chair in Media Studies in the English Department of the University of Virginia in Richmond, where she directs a new program in media studies focusing on developing a critical and historical understanding of the cultural effects of traditional and new media.

Rae Ekman is a master calligrapher and artist. She moved to Los Angeles to study under the tutelage of Rabbi Tauber, whose weekly seminars led her to take notes each week and make those notes meditations on handling life at the end of the 20th century. Her calm and peace are a product of these learnings.

Evelyn Eller of Forest Hills, New York was educated at the School of Visual Arts in New York City, Pratt Graphic Center, and the Art Students League, among other institutions. She has been in countless group shows throughout the world and has had solo shows for the past 18 years. Being a traveler, she incorporates her experiences in "travel" bookworks.

Dorothy Field of Cobble Hill, British Columbia in Canada grew up in an assimilated family in New York in a town where being Jewish seemed totally normal. When she moved to a farm in rural Canada, she found herself living at the edge of the Diaspora. Trying to educate herself to figure out what "Jewishness" meant, she sees that the core of orientation of her Jewishness grows out of the idea of *tikkun olam*, the repair of the world. In her work, she tries to speak out even when it feels risky and to work towards integration of the shadow side, the Other, the Jew, on a personal and political level. She has studied handmade papermaking and taught at Paper & Book Intensive. She lectures widely on Asian paper and has been in many exhibitions.

Diane Fine is Associate Professor of Art at Plattsburgh State University of New York, having graduated in Graphic Arts emphasizing printmaking and the book arts from the University of Wisconsin-Madison. She is proprietor of the Moonkosh Press and is represented in collections including the New York Public Library, the Museum of Modern Art in New York and the Yale University Art Gallery. The source of *Forever and Ever* is the desire to understand the role that Judaism plays in coping with breast cancer in her family, her sister Beth having been diagnosed over 4 years ago. As the sisters read and talked to their rabbis and to each other, they found wonder, comfort, and a shared challenge in learning to wear teffilin (the metaphor of the sealed box as container for the answers). Their study, and this book, has enlightened them with its message of healing.

Rose-Lynn Fisher, a graduate of Otis Art Institute in Los Angeles, is a photographer who has traveled widely for the Consulate General of Israel in Los Angeles and for the Center for Jewish Culture and Creativity. She is represented in many public collections throughout the world and has been recipient of many grants and residencies.

Faiya Fredman of La Jolla, California was educated at UCLA. She has had many solo shows, as well as participating in several group shows. She is known for her photography, her installations, as well as her public works. Her bookworks reside in many public collections.

Pnina Gagnon, an Israeli/Canadian artist, has had many solo shows both in Canada and in Israel, where she resides part of every year. She has also been in countless group exhibitions since 1967. A passionate and committed artist, Gagnon studied at the Ecole des Beaux-Arts in the sixties, and has been very active in many solo ehxibitions, as well as group shows and has created 7 artist books. In Israel, she has participated in solo shows at the National Marine Museum and in the Museum of Ein Harod. In 1995, she participated in an important group show of Eight Women for Peace in the Museum of Haifa. Her works are in many public and private collections in Canada and in Israel. This is the first time her work has been seen in the United States. The book she has in the show, *Man at Work*, shows her father building a structure, and the accompanying scroll is in Hebrew letters but contains Yiddish, Arabic and Hebrew.

Vered Galor, a photographer and teacher of photography living in Woodland Hills, California, was born in Czechoslovakia and grew up in Israel. She has been a glass sculptor, then turned to art consulting and independent curating. A lecturer and facilitator, she returned to studio work choosing photography as a departure point. Her bookwork relates the history of her parents during World War II during the Nazi regime, her own beginnings, and leads up to the war of 1967, from war to war. It is powerful and ingenious.

Ruth Ginsberg-Place, who lives in Boston, is a graduate of Syracuse University with an M.F.A. and of Simmons School of Social Work with a Master of Social Work. She has been in exhibitions for over 25 years and is a photographer and printmaker.

Sylvia Glass of Woodland Hills, California makes bookworks of the humblest materials including rocks, fossils, twigs and a myriad of found objects. She recently had a retrospective at the Jan Baum Gallery in Los Angeles.

Alisa Golden of Northern California is the proprietor of never mind the press, where she has written, designed, printed, and bound more than 50 editions with approximately 10 per cent devoted to distinctly Jewish themes. Books and broadsides from never mind the press can be found in the special collections departments of universities and libraries including Skirball Museum, Hebrew Union College, Houghton Library at Harvard University; etc.

Beth Grossman of Northern California is a painter, arts organizer, theater artist, as well as a graphic designer. With an MFA in Performance Studies, she has studied in Malaysia, Oslo, Norway, and Tianjin, China. She has participated in countless exhibitions of her project, *Passages: Jewish Women's Immigration and Family History*, a six-room temporary public art installation.

c.j. grossman, a San Francisco resident, has an MFA from California College of Arts and Crafts. She has participated in many group exhibitions and has been a teacher of art and master binder for many years. Socially conscious, grossman has explored her Jewish roots in relation to her lifelong commitment to struggle for civil rights for all people. Her work is a bridge between education and understanding among people.

Carol Hamoy of New York City has had solo exhibitions for the past twenty years, and has also participated in many group shows. A product of the Art Students League, Hamoy has developed her art from a feminist point of view and has consistently used Jewish themes in her work, dealing with ethereal messages and universal truths. She often uses artifacts from the garment industry which allude to her family's work.

Gloria Helfgott, now of Southern California, but formerly from Connecticut, is an expert in bookmaking and binding and has been an important educator both in the East and now on the West Coast for techniques in bookmaking. She brings exquisite craftsmanship with significant content in her bookworks. She has also curated many exhibitions on the East as well as on the West Coast.

Judy Hoffman of Brooklyn, New York, is renowned for her environmental installations, which are explosions of fantastical concoctions. She has been in many group shows and has an admirable record of solo shows as well. She is a performance artist, as well as a recipient of several commissions. She also teaches and gives workshops. Among her work are artist books with Judaic themes which appear in this exhibition. Her work is handmade from combinations of paper pulp, wire, and scavenged materials.

Sandra Jackman of New York City has been exhibiting bookworks, assemblage, and collage for many years. She has worked in collections throughout the United States. Her emphasis on bookworks stems from her wide reading and her ability to transfer information into sculptural constructions in book form.

Jacqueline Jacobs was born in Chile but now is a pediatrician in La Jolla, California. She is the wife of a physician and mother of two physicians. She has been in many exhibitions in California, with works in ceramic, sculpture, weaving and textile design, as well as bookworks. Her dual careers in Healing and the Visual Arts are complementary.

Sue Abbe Kaplan is the proprietor of Shulamis Press in Venice, California, begun in the fall of 1996; its mission is to bring to print works that explore Jewish themes in limited editions using traditional fine-press production methods, hand set-metal type, and a Vandercook cylinder press. Kaplan is a researcher in early printed books of 16th-century Venice, so she is influenced by the look and feel of those beautiful books, the classic proportions of the page layout and of the types used. This is the first book of the Shulamis Press. Future projects include modern Jewish-American poetry and medieval fables.

Tatana Kellner was born in Prague, Czechoslovakia but is now a resident of Kingston, New York where she has directed the Women's Studio Workshop in Rosendale, New York for over 25 years. She has an MFA from Rochester Institute of Technology and a BA from the University of Toledo. She has created many artist books, and her work is in many public collections. The volumes in this exhibition are the story of her mother and her father, both survivors of the Holocaust. They are iconic and are truly seminal to this exhibition.

Karen Klein of Cambridge, MA is a professor at Brandeis University and has appeared in many groups shows, as well as solo exhibitions. She is very influenced by literature in her visual work which includes sculpture, as well as works on paper.

Lisa Kokin is a self-taught Richmond, California artist who makes bookworks in order to express herself through images and layers of meaning through the incorporation of found objects such as phrases, maps, buttons, pictures, and other fabrics. Re-discovering her Jewish heritage has allowed Kokin to turn to the medium most associated with the "People of the Book." She has had many one-person exhibitions, as well as participating in many group shows. *Six Books* are Hebrew books which are exhibited as mangled books covered with cowgut and acrylic medium. The books were a reaction to Kokin's visit to Buchenwald. She also has a keen sense of humor and *Babes in Goyland* bring out a cunning and smile which can only be realized by someone Jewish who teaches in a Catholic school.

Elaine Langerman is a Washington, DC artist, graduate of the American University and the University of Maryland. She has been in several one-person exhibitions, as well as group shows for more than 20 years. She is a painter and bookmaker, whose *Sefer* consists of woven paper pages to signify how the sacred and profane are woven together in our lives, and how we intertwine our lives with each other. Her palette is joyous and bright, mostly using acrylic paints, and she tries to create realms of enchantment for the heart where it might find play and adventure.

Stephanie Later is a major bookbinder and artist, a graduate of Syracuse University School of Fine Arts, Parsons and the Art Students League of New York. First an illustrator and window display designer, she turned to bookmaking and especially bookbinding, receiving a New York State grant for the conservation of books at the Metropolitan Museum of Art. Her *Song of Songs* is the result of intense research of collections of illuminated manuscripts, and this particular subject matter has biblical, historical, and sentimental significance. Each page is hand calligraphed and illustrated using gouache and gold acrylic paint. The illustrations depict the fervent love of King Solomon and his wife. The bookwork is housed in a box of cut-out wooden boards with inlays of faux ivory panels and some semi-precious and glass stones. She lives in NewYork City.

Stephanie Brody Lederman has her studio in Brooklyn and has been seen in solo exhibitions since 1976. She has also been in a myriad of group shows throughout the East Coast. She has been the recipient of many grants and awards and is widely collected in many public collections throughout the world. She is known as a narrative artist.

May Lesser comes from a family of physicians, and most of her work has been produced within medical institutions. From time spent at the UCLA Medical School, USC County General Hospital, Tulane University Medical Center and the Charity Hospital in New Orleans, she has developed trust of the physicians, and this is reflected in her art. From working in this setting for 30 years, her pictures both reflect her own artistic evolution and document the changes and continuities in modern medicine. Much of her work has been influenced by Rubens, Rembrandt, and their Biblical paintings. She has been in exhibitions throughout the country, for the past 50 years, and is a painter, printmaker and graphic artist. She resides in New Orleans, LA.

Paula Levine is a Canadian-American visual artist whose works in video, photography, and installation have been widely shown in the U.S. and Canada, although never in a solo Bay Area exhibition, where she lives. Levine's writings on installation have been published in the Banff Art Center's *Radio Rethink* and in several journals. She teaches in the Conceptual Design and Photography Departments at San Francisco State University, and the Photography Departments at San Francisco State University the San Francisco Art Institute. She has a series of bookworks which use the Old and New Testament a subject and object, called *as if the laws were malleable*, using the Bible to investigate questions of tradition, conventions and protocol in relation to Judaism, feminism, and the politics of everyday. The series was begun in 1991 and still continues, numbering over 62 pieces.

Levine also has a series called *Burials and Borders*, which is a project on history and memory, and the construction of the one through the other. Situated in Israel, with a focus on the Golan Heights, this is a portrait of the Golan made at a time of transition as Israel sturggles toward peace with Syria.

Liliane Lijn is a renowned artist who as an American lives in England, recipient of countless public art commissions as a sculptor. In the midst of her sculptural works, she also has on occasion created books which resonate with personal and autobiographical elements. Among these are *Her Mother's Voice*, the first volume in an autobiographical trilogy, which she is generated on her own computer. Always experimental, Lijn has created extremely beautiful works of art on the printing press and now on her computer.

Jenni Lukac spent a residency in Portugal to study the history of the Crypto-Jews still living in that country. She also has created a series of artist books, collage and video installations which addressed the personal narrative of, and the political persecutions against Jews in Europe in the 1930's and 40's. Formerly from Virginia, she now travels and resides with her husband wherever he is assigned.

Joan Lyons is a co-founder of the Visual Studies Workshop Press, where she has been mentoring artists into making printed books for almost three decades. She also has published several of her own bookworks, which have been autobiographical or feminist in flavor. She has been a leader in the movement of printed artist books and many artists owe her a salute for all the work she has done to further the publication of multiples throughout the past generation.

Lyons has made work in a variety of media including silver-gelatin prints, artists' books, archaic photographic processes, pinhole photography, offset lithography, photo-quiltmaking and computer-based work. In the current series of digital prints "Re-Presentations," Lyons has been photographing historical painting and sculpture, as well as more recently constructed images, in an attempt to isolate and reframe the major project of Western art—the representation of men and women.

Barbara Magnus lives in Los Angeles and creates labor-intensive installations and bookworks. *Bible for a New World* is actually an English-German dictionary from 1897. She is known to alter the literal and the practical to expose the book's subtext through form. These "wheels" and the extreme "dog-eared" fold of the pages refer to repeated use, marking one's place, and assimilating the new while holding onto the old. This dictionary was a compromise for her relatives to find an English-Yiddish dictionary. In addition to vocabulary, grammar, usage and useful phrases, are letters and customary responses concerning personal and business circumstances of the day.

Judith Margolis of Jerusalem, Israel studied at Columbia University and Cooper Union in New York City. She began making limited edition artist books in 1969. She moved to Los Angeles and received an MFA from University of Southern California in painting and film graphics. She has recently made aliya to Israel with her husband David and daughter Hodya. She has recently founded Bright Idea Books, a Jerusalem-based publishing company devoted to producing limited edition artist books and contemporary fiction.

Kathi Martin of West Hills, California trained in printmaking at the University of Washington and then having received an MFA in Studio Art, she began teaching at Taft High School and at California State University, Northridge. She incorporates found objects, stitchery, and appropriated imagery into her work. Her connection with her grandmother, Eva Michelson, and her connection with Yiddish meld in this Bubby book, which shows the richness of her experiences as a Jewish girl, going to Temple, summer camp, and having a cousin as a Rabbi. But what a grandmother, who is historified through the memories of her artist-grandchild!

Barbara Milman of Davis, California was formerly a lawyer for 25 years, defending the civil rights of American citizens. Barbara Milman is a printmaker and mixed media artist whose work addresses feminism, Jewish identity, and other political and cultural issues. She has been shown widely throughout the United States, and is represented in many museums and public collections. In 1997 Milman published prints, emphasizing interviews with Holocaust survivors, creating each story with 12 prints, constituting a chapter of the book, *Shadow of Death*, a limited edition bookwork. All 60 of the prints have been included in a paperback book, *Light in the Shadows*, published in 1997 by Jonathan David Publisher.

Beverly Naidus of Shelburne Falls, MA was a professor at California State University, Long Beach before moving to Massachusetts. A socially aware and politically active artist, Naidus has created a bookwork that looks at secular/cultural Jewish identity in relation to assimilation, using scanned images from old magazines and an old photo of immigrants on a boat.

Miriam Neiger of Jerusalem was born in Slovakia and came to Israel in 1949. A graduate of Bezalel Art Academy, she has exhibited many one-person shows as well as group exhibitions throughout North American and Israel. She is also a poet.

Wendy Oberlander, a Canadian who lives in Vancouver, created a prize-winning video called *Nothing to be written here*, about Jewish immigration to Canada. She has been an artist-educator and teacher, curated exhibitions, received many grants and residencies and participated in group exhibitions as well as solo exhibitions in California and in Canada. She is for the most part an installation artist.

Laurel Paley has an MFA from Claremont Graduate School and a BA from Smith College. She is an expert in calligraphy as well as digital media. Having appeared in many solo exhibitions as well as group shows, she is also a faculty member of several colleges in the Southern California area. She is a painter, printmaker, and bookmaker.

Io Palmer a recent MFA graduate from the University of Arizona in Tucson, worked with Gayle Wimmer, professor in the Art Department who is also in Women of the Book, and has created a body of work that reflects her own diversity, having a Jewish mother and an African-American father. Her clay book forms celebrate all the members of her family on both sides, and Aunt Ruth is one of Palmer's favorite relatives, and thus the bookwork in this exhibition.

Vaughan Rachel has also worked on a number of community projects with arts and public service organizations in the Los Angeles area. She is a convert to Judaism, who married artist Allan Kaprow in 1955, and converted at that time when she took the Hebrew name Rachel as her own. Her being Jewish is everything to do with her life and her art; there is no separation.

Sonya Rapoport of Berkeley, California is one of the first artists to have combined art and science in computer works, which she created in the early 1970s. Her printout pieces have made her renowned throughout the United States, and now she is a digital artist creating work for the WEB, yet she always comes back to the "book" which she has re-defined with digital technology and inventive humor. Much of her work has been "interactive" before the term was even applied to bookworks. Yet, she invites always the participation of the viewer/reader in all her works. *The Transgenic Bagel* is a participatory bookwork, made especially for this exhibition. You can read this bookwork also on http://www.lanminds.com/local/sr/srbagel.html

Eva-Lynn Ratoff has been a calligrapher of great note since 1976, combining her great talents with bookbinding, papermaking, marbling, and painting. Inspired by Torah, prayers, songs, and images, her work expresses her feelings about Judaism. She is the official scribe of Temple Ahavat Shalom and has exhibited in many galleries in the Southern California area. She feels that with words and color, her art reflects her soul, bringing to others moments of spirituality and reminding people what it is to be a Jew. She resides in Northridge, California.

Gail Rebhan is Director of Media Technology Studies at Trinity College in Washington, DC. Her work is in many public collections including the Corcoran Gallery of Art, National Museum of American Art, J. Paul Getty Museum, and Polaroid Corporation. She produced an artist's book, *Mother-Son Talk,* at Visual Studies Workshop in Rochester, NY. Her work is included in several other books including the anthology *Reframings:New American Feminist Photographies* and *Our Grandmothers: Photographs by 75 Women Photographers.* Exhibitions include: Corcoran Gallery of Art, Washington, DC; Folkwang Museum, Essen, Germany; School 33 Art Center, Baltimore, Maryland. Rebhan has an M.F.A. from California Institute of the Arts.

Marilyn Rosenberg of Peekskill, New York has been making bookworks for many years, having been included in many group exhibitions as well as solo shows. This is one of the first years that Rosenberg has been involved in Jewish themes, but one was a Ketubah for her younger daughter. This bookwork on Babi Yar, commemorates the massacre of murdered Jewish women in Russia.

Sophia Rosenberg of Victoria, British Columbia (Canada) is a graduate of the University of Victoria. She is involved in papermaking, bookmaking, mask making, and various painting techniques. She is also a published poet and author/illustrator of a children's book. *The Lilith Scroll* is a collaborative work, which has a great resonance for this exhibition.

Marleene Rubenstein has recently received an MFA from California State University, Long Beach, and has participated in drawing and print shows, but this is her first bookwork exhibition, in which she has evoked loss and grief. She resides in Los Angeles.

Linda Rubinstein lives in Putney, Vermont and is the director at the Brattleboro Museum. She is a graduate of Hunter College. She and her sister, Judith Stein, grew up in a Jewish family with a mother who was an artist. Rubinstein has been making one-of-a-kind bookworks for many years and has been in many group exhibitions, as well as solo exhibitions in New England.

Rochelle Rubinstein is a Canadian book artist who makes bookworks with hand-written texts in Hebrew and in English, adding woodcuts, linocuts, rubberstamps, and silkscreened prints and copy art. Her images serve as a contemporary and feminist counterpoint for biblical texts, such as *Book of Ruth*, *Book of Esther*, *Song of Songs*, and *Lamentations*, the book in this exhibition. She has exhibited since 1984 and has received numerous commissions and grants.

Alyssa C. Salomon of Richmond, Virginia has an MBA from University of Chicago and a BA from Kenyon College in Gambier, Ohio. Her background is in textile art, from which her one-of-a-kind bookworks have evolved as visual poems.

Robyn Sassen lives in Johannesburg, South Africa having a BA in Fine Arts and an MA in Art History from the University of South Africa. She has had several solo exhibitions, as well as commissions. Being a woman and a Jew in South Africa creates a number of intersecting dynamics, of both a political and an intellectual nature, within which she perceives herself and allows herself to continue to work.

Claire J. Satin of Dania, Florida is renowned throughout the South largely for her bookworks and her public art commissions, many allied to new libraries including alphawalks and sculptures of alphabet letters. Her use of tough materials such as metal in her bookworks, as well as lyrical alphabetical designs in her public works makes her signature pieces welcome pieces which are integrated into architectural settings.

Miriam Schaer of Brooklyn, New York is a teacher who has made bookworks for many years, appearing in countless one-person and group exhibitions. Her bookworks tend to be kinetic sculptures created with papers, fabrics, beads, and objects. *Eve's Meditation* is in the form of a serpent, a book, and a fruit, the shape of which fills the serpent with the spirit of hidden knowledge. In *Eve's Meditation*, the path to knowing is through the belly of the snake. Knowledge is dangerous and apart, allied with temptation, acquired in disobedience, and published by shame-all signs of the significance of the outsider, the guest denied the feast, and characteristic of her own relationship to Judaism.

Helen Schamroth of Auckland, New Zealand was born in Crakow, Poland. Her remarkable bookwork, *New World, Old Story*, tells her life's story from Poland to Europe to Melbourne, where she grew up, married a New Zealander, and moved to Auckland. She has three daughters, two of whom are gourmet chefs, and the other a journalist in London. She was invited to install a Holocaust Memorial piece in the room dedicated to the Holocaust in the Auckland City Art Gallery, which recently opened. She has written and lectured about arts and crafts and has published a book about crafts in New Zealand.

Arleen Schloss is a multimedia artist of New York City, who has created many video works throughout the past 25 years. The bookwork she has included in this exhibition was a seminal work in early Xerography and has resonance even to this day.

Mira Schor of New York City is known for her painting and her writing. As co-editor of *M/E/A/N/I/N/G* with Susan Bee, another artist in this exhibition, she made a great contribution to the intersection between politics and art in which artists, art historians, poets, and critics found a place to challenge the theoretical and commercial hegemony in the contemporary cultural ecology. Being a painter who loves language, the bookwork she has created for this exhibition reflects the intelligence and the humor which the visualization of language can produce. Schor teaches at Parsons School of Design.

Judith Serebrin of Northern California was educated at the University of Utah and has participated in exhibitions of art books and prints since 1992. She has gravitated to the form of scrolls and books since 1990.

Joyce Cutler Shaw is a multimedia artist, including drawings, installations, public projects, and artist books. She has exhibited internationally since 1972. Her *Alphabet of Bones* is an original calligraphy inspired by the hollow bones of birds and conceived as a visual dance. Its 26 double characters have been digitized and can be translated into the English alphabet, as well as a symbolic code.

Her extended visual narrative, *The Mesenger Cycle* (1975-90) has been followed by the current series, *The Anatomy Lesson*, an investigation of human identity and the evolving self from birth through death, with the body as the matrix of the human condition. She is the first visual artist to be appointed Artist-in-Residence, as a Visiting Scholar (1992-2000), by the School of Medicine at the University of California, San Diego and the first visual artist nationally to have such a medical school residency. She has as her goal to realize a contemporary re-vision of a traditional theme, *The Anatomy Lesson*. Her work is represented in both museum and library special collections throughout the country and abroad. She resides in La Jolla, California.

Karen Shaw lives in Baldwin, New York, the product of a very secular Jewish household. She has been making bookworks for many years and has explored the cabalistic system of Gematria which is the number/language system exhibited in her bookworks.

Genie Shenk, a California artist, received her MFA from UCLA in 1990. Since then, she has taught book arts at the Athenaeum Library in La Jolla and at San Diego Mesa College, where she is co-founder of Mesa Arts Press, a student letterpress facility. She has conducted numerous lectures and workshops and was a project coordinator for INSITE'97. Her work has been widely shown and is currently included in "Dreams 1900 -2000," travelling internationally. She is represented in many library collections, including that of the University of California, San Diego, and the National Museum of Women in the Arts.

Elena Siff lives in Santa Monica, California as a major assemblage artist, who has appeared in many exhibitions throughout the country, as well as being a curator of many book, assemblage, and mail art exhibitions. She is also the co-curator of the international exhibition, *Women Beyond Borders*. Her bookwork, *Rootless: On the Road with my Jewish Half*, is the result of a personal journey for her, to put her in touch with her long-departed grandparents and their three sons, one of whom was her fascinating father, Philip, who basically ignored his Jewish identity for all of her life with him. Finding letters, documents, articles that her father left her, when he died on her birthday in 1981, she has reconstructed the great tragedy in her father's life. She has used an old toy truck as her bookform; the pages are the truck's cargo, and the content is the actual photos, letters and documents that she has discovered on the journey back to her Jewish half.

Jenny Snider, a graduate of Yale University, is an Associate Professor of Fine Arts at Queens College. A resident of New York City, Snider is a painter and teacher.

Franca Sonnino lives in Rome, Italy and has had many solo exhibitions, as well as group shows. She has been a painter, but has also done many bookworks, involved herself in many mail art exhibitions, as well as textile shows.

Leah Sosewitz of Highland Park, Illinois is an accomplished calligrapher, who creates ketubot, illuminations, and papercuts.

Victoria Stanton is a Montreal-based interdisciplinary artist working in a variety of media including spoken word performance performance intervention (site specific work), self-publishing, and sound recording. She has participated in exhibitions of bookworks and mail art, mostly in Canada and in New York City. Her bookworks are generally collage and text, photocopied, either hand sewn or spiral bound. The bookwork in this exhibition was made especially for *Women of the Book*.

Ursula Sternberg was a bookmaker and painter who participated in exhibitions since 1983 in Paris, Brussels, Dusseldorf, Zurich, Frankfurt, London, Cologne, and the United States. A Philadelphia resident, she passed away in late September 2000.

Carrie Ungerman, Los Angeles-based, draws attention to the details of daily life by placing them in a different context. Often her process and work employ the making, collecting and/or the amassing of the materials and objects for a project. Her studying of text in both traditional and non-traditional settings, as well her cumulative life experiences studying and teaching, both influence and inform her work.

She has shown in group shows since 1985 and has exhibited in solo and smaller shows since 1988. She serves as Visual Arts Director for the Brandeis-Bardin Institute, a Jewish educational and cultural institution in Simi Valley.

Lila Wahrhaftig is a multifaceted artist who works in handmade paper objects, intaglio prints, and more recently with letterforms, which allowed her to create this computer generated bookwork. She has exhibited in California for the past 25 years.

Ruth Wallen of San Diego, California is a lecturer at University of California, San Diego at La Jolla. She has done several public art commissions, has had solo ehibitions/performances, has been in many group exhibitions, has been a Fulbright Scholar in the Mexico Border Lectures Program, and has worked with Las Comadres on the California-Mexico border.

Ellen Wallenstein-Sea lives in New York City, and has an MFA in Photography from Pratt Institute and a BA in Art History from SUNY at Stony Brook, New York. She has been a photo archivist for several agencies in New York, and taught at the University of Texas at Austin. She has curated several exhibitions and is in several public collections.

Ruth Weisberg is the Dean of the School of Fine Arts at the University of Southern California in Los Angeles, former president of the Women's Caucus for Art, former president of the College Art Association, and noted printmaker and painter. Born in Chicago, educated at the University of Michigan, with a stint at the Accademia di Belle Art in Perugia, Italy, Weisberg went to Paris and spent six months at Stanley William Hayter's printmaking Atelier 17 in 1964. In 1969 she moved to Santa Monica, California and a year later began teaching at University of Southern California. She was the first woman to serve as president of the College Art Association (1990).

Gayle Wimmer lives in Tucson, Arizona, where she is a professor of Art at the University of Arizona. She has been a visiting Fulbright Professor in Haifa, Israel and has had an International Research Grant to do research on contemporary artists in Poland since 1971. She has been in many group exhibitions in North America, Poland, and Bulgaria.

Thanks

There are so many people to thank, but first of all, I must thank the artists not only for their contributions to this exhibition, but also for their moral support, their physical efforts in helping to install, take photographs, take slides, and spread the word about this most important exhibition. You all know who you are, and I am infinitely grateful to you.

To the directors of each venue and their staffs (if they do have staff), I must express my gratitude for complete cooperation, collaboration, and support. You all have offered up venues that have been flexible and dynamic spaces for the bookworks in this exhibition. Students and friends have contributed in making the installation a marvelous experience. Your communities have also helped to make this exhibition significant.

To Channa Horwitz, Diane Calder, and Vered Galor, thank you for all your photographic skills; and to Barbara Drucker, John O'Brien and Harry Reese thank you for logistical help.

I must thank the embracing support of Florida Atlantic University, not only to Rod Faulds who made this exhibition shimmer in the Ritter Art Gallery in Boca Raton, but also to the staff of Special Collections in the Wimberly Library, especially Nancine Thompson and Zita Cael, who made this catalog possible as a publication of the Friends of the Library; to Mary Dean, who helped find financial support for this catalog; and to Dr. William Miller, who forwarded the cause of this publication to its realization.

Thanks to Bruce Brown, who believed in this catalog and demonstrated that belief with contributions to help pay for the design and production of this catalog. And thanks especially to James Wintner, who offered to put a selection of this exhibition on the Internet, to allow many more people to appreciate and understand the importance of this exhibition. Even today, you can see part of the exhibition at http://colophon.com/gallery and eventually you will be able to see much of the catalog online. To Jim, we owe so very much.

Above all, I must thank my sister, Esther Liu, who has given me moral support in making this exhibition a significant chapter in my life. She has sustained it in every way to demonstrate how much it means to her as well as to me. In the midst of problems and progress, she has been there for me through thick and thin, and I am eternally grateful.

And of course, thanks to Linda Rubinstein, who was the catalyst for this exhibition. Without her bookworks, I would never have been driven to do this exhibition, which has enlightened many thousands of visitors, but which has also expanded my own vistas into my own culture. Thank you also goes to the many active visitors to the exhibition who have contributed additional information to enhance my understanding of how deeply this exhibition has touched their hearts and souls.

I also would like to thank Maritta Tapanainen and Patrick Percy who have designed this catalog with skill and understanding and have helped so much to make this a design event as well as a book exhibition.

jah